The 20th Century's
MOST INFLUENTIAL
HISPANICS

Pelé
Soccer Superstar

by Laurie Collier Hillstrom

LUCENT BOOKS
An imprint of Thomson Gale, a part of The Thomson Corporation

THOMSON
GALE

Detroit • New York • San Francisco • New Haven, Conn. • Waterville, Maine • London

LIBRARY OF CONGRESS CATALOGING-IN-PUBLICATION DATA

Hillstrom, Laurie Collier, 1965–
    Pelé : soccer superstar / by Laurie Collier Hillstrom.
      p. cm. — (The twentieth century's most influential Hispanics)
  Includes bibliographical references and index.
  ISBN 978-1-4205-0023-3 (hardcover)
    1. Pelé, 1940—Juvenile literature. 2. Soccer players—Brazil—Biography—Juvenile literature. I. Title.
  GV942.7.P42H55 2008
  796.334092—dc22
                                                                                      2007032108

ISBN-10: 1-4205-0023-6
Printed in the United States of America

Table of Contents

Foreword

When Alberto Gonzales was a boy living in Texas, he never dreamed he would one day stand next to the president of the United States. Born to poor migrant workers, Gonzales grew up in a two-bedroom house shared by his family of ten. There was no telephone or hot water. Because his parents were too poor to send him to college, Gonzales joined the Air Force, but after two years obtained an appointment to the Air Force Academy and, from there, transferred to Rice University. College was still a time of struggle for Gonzales, who had to sell refreshments in the bleachers during football games to support himself. But he eventually went on to Harvard Law School and rose to prominence in the Texas government. And then one day, decades after rising from his humble beginnings in Texas, he found himself standing next to President George W. Bush at the White House. The president had nominated him to be the nation's first Hispanic attorney general. As he accepted the nomination, Gonzales embraced the president and said, "'Just give me a chance to prove myself'—that is a common prayer for those in my community. Mr. President, thank you for that chance."

Like Gonzales, many Hispanics in America and elsewhere have shed humble beginnings to soar to impressive and previously unreachable heights. In the twenty-first century, influential Hispanic figures can be found worldwide and in all fields of endeavor including science, politics, education, the arts, sports, religion and literature. Some accomplishments, like those of musician Carlos Santana or author Alisa Valdes-Rodriguez, have added a much-needed Hispanic voice to the artistic landscape. Others, such as revolutionary Che Guevara or labor leader Dolores Huerta, have spawned international social movements that have enriched the rights of all peoples.

But who exactly is Hispanic? When studying influential Hispanics, it is important to understand what the term actually means. Unlike strictly racial categories like "black" or "Asian," the term "Hispanic" joins a huge swath of people from different countries, religions, and races. The category was first used by the U.S. census bureau in 1980 and is used to refer to Spanish-speaking people of any race. Officially, it denotes a person whose ancestry either descends in whole or in part from the people of Spain or the various peoples of Spanish-speaking Latin America. Often the term "Hispanic" is used synonymously with the term "Latino," but the two actually have slightly different meanings. "Latino" refers only to people from the countries of Latin America, such as Argentina, Brazil, and Venezuela, whether they speak Spanish or Portuguese. Meanwhile, Hispanic refers to only Spanish-speaking peoples but from any Spanish-speaking country, such as Spain, Puerto Rico or Mexico.

In America, Hispanics are reaching new heights of cultural influence, buying power, and political clout. More than 35 million people identified themselves as Hispanic on the 2000 U.S. census, and there were estimated to be more than 41 million Hispanics in America as of 2006. In the twenty-first century people of Hispanic origin have officially become the nation's largest ethnic minority, outnumbering blacks and Asians. Hispanics constitute about 13 percent of the nation's total population, and by 2050 their numbers are expected to rise to 102.6 million, at which point they would account for 24 percent of the total population. With growing numbers and expanding influence, Hispanic leaders, artists, politicians, and scientists in America and in other countries are commanding attention like never before.

These unique and fascinating stories are the subjects of *The Twentieth Century's Most Influential Hispanics* collection from Lucent Books. Each volume in the series critically examines the challenges, accomplishments, and legacy of influential Hispanic figures, many of whom, like Alberto Gonzales, sprang from modest beginnings to achieve groundbreaking goals. *The Twentieth Century's Most Influential Hispanics* offers vivid narrative, fully documented primary and secondary source quotes, a bibliography, thorough index, and mix of color and black and white photographs which enhance each volume and provide excellent starting points for research and discussion.

The King of Soccer

Brazil's Edson Arantes do Nascimento, better known as Pelé, is widely thought to be the greatest soccer player in history. "It is almost meaningless to call Pelé incomparable or peerless or to use any other of the terms that glorify an athlete's ability," said a writer for the *New York Times*. "The name Pelé itself has become an adjective for [greatness]."[1]

Pelé's remarkable playing career lasted for twenty years, from 1957 to 1977. During that time he led Brazil's national team to three World Cup titles—in 1958, 1962, and 1970—and scored a record ninety-seven career goals in international competition. Pelé also starred for the Santos professional team in Brazil and for the New York Cosmos of the North American Soccer League. Pelé scored an amazing 1,281 goals during his long career, the highest number of goals in the modern era of professional soccer. To put this achievement into perspective, sports analysts have compared it to a major league baseball star hitting seventy home runs per season for twenty years.

Pelé also revolutionized the sport of soccer. His speed, vision, and creative play-making skills made Brazil famous for its attacking style of offense and helped to make the game more exciting

Pelé's fame as a soccer player got him an appearance on Johnny Carson's Tonight show.

for casual fans. "Pelé was the greatest of them all," declared a writer for the International Football Hall of Fame Web site.

> He was lithe, agile, strong, and seemed to be able to make the ball do as he pleased. Blessed with a stunning shot and an ability to soar above defenses, he was expected to perform some astonishing feat of trickery every time he was in possession.[2]

Although Pelé is clearly one of the greatest soccer players of all time, he became equally well-known and respected for his contributions off the field. His life story, which was featured in several books and movies, has inspired millions of people around the world. Born in a small village in Brazil's interior, Pelé was too poor to afford shoes as a boy and learned to play soccer by kicking a sock stuffed with rags through the dusty streets. Through talent, determination, hard work, and a passion for soccer, he overcame these circumstances to achieve tremendous wealth and fame. "There is a sense that Pelé belongs more to global heritage than he does to Brazil's," noted a soccer historian. "He is an international reference point, and one who is simple to understand: a poor black man who became the best in the world through dedication and skill."[3]

After his playing career ended, Pelé became a world representative for his beloved sport of soccer. He believed that soccer allowed people to overcome their differences and that the sport had the power to promote peace, understanding, and goodwill. "To bring soccer to the countries where soccer is undeveloped, this is my passion," he explained. "I want to see soccer all over the world. All people can be part of it."[4]

Chapter 1

Talent Overcomes Obstacles

Pelé showed an amazing ability as a soccer player from an early age. His skill and dedication to the game helped him to overcome a number of obstacles—including poverty and a very limited education—to launch one of the most successful careers in modern sports history.

An Early Interest in Soccer

Pelé was born on October 23, 1940, in the poor village of Três Corações in central Brazil. His mother, Celeste, and father, Joaõ Ramos do Nascimento, named him Edson Arantes do Nascimento. They chose the name Edson because they admired the American scientist Thomas Edison, who invented the electric light bulb. Edson's friends would later nickname him Pelé.

Edson's father was also known by a nickname. He played professional soccer under the name Dondinho and was known as a promising young player until a knee injury cut short his career. Under his father's influence, Edson developed an early interest in soccer (better known outside the United States as football). "Football was the only career I ever thought of," he said. "I wanted

Pelé's name given at birth was Edson, because his parents admired American scientist Thomas Edison.

to follow my father. I thought he was the greatest soccer player who ever lived. He just never got a chance to prove it."[5]

Since his family could not afford to buy a soccer ball, Edson made his own by stuffing an old sock with rags or crumpled newspapers. The size and weight of this makeshift ball changed often, depending on the type of stuffing available and whether conditions were wet or dry. Edson spent much of his free time kicking this stuffed sock up and down the narrow, dusty street in front of his house. "The pleasure of kicking that ball, making it move, making it respond to an action of mine, was the greatest feeling of power I had ever had up to that time,"[6] he recalled.

A Mother's Expectations

While Pelé's father taught him how to play soccer, his mother taught him how to be a good person. Celeste Nascimento ran a strict but loving household. She expected her children to obey her rules and treat other people with respect. Whenever Pelé failed to meet his mother's expectations, he received a swat on the ear or a spanking. "Her code was rigid," Pelé remembered in his autobiography. "The Arantes do Nascimento family were poor, but we behaved. We didn't steal, we didn't beg, we didn't lie, we didn't cheat, we didn't use swear words regardless of the provocation.... And above all, we obeyed our parents—or else!"

Pelé, with Robert L. Fish, *My Life and the Beautiful Game*. Garden City, New York: Doubleday, 1977, p. 17.

Edson was born in a poor Brazilian village much like this one.

Poor boys in Brazil, like Edson, loved to play soccer, even if they had no shoes or proper ball.

Struggling with Poverty

Although Edson found a way to play soccer despite his family's circumstances, poverty still affected his life in many ways. When he was six years old, Edson's family moved to Baurú, a larger town in southern Brazil, in hopes of improving their circumstances. Edson's father played soccer for the local Baurú Athletic Club (BAC) team and also worked as an assistant in a health clinic. But Dondinho barely earned enough money to support the family. By this time Edson had a younger brother, Jair (known to his family and friends as Zoca), and a younger sister, Maria Lúcia. The Nascimentos also sometimes shared their home with an uncle, a grandmother, and other members of their extended family.

In Baurú, the Nascimento family lived in a rented house with a leaky roof, and they had to huddle around a wood-burning stove to stay warm in the winter. Edson and the other children wore hand-me-down clothing and usually went barefoot because they could not afford to buy shoes. Edson's parents spent a lot of time worrying about whether they would have enough money to buy food. "Poverty is a curse that depresses the mind, drains the spirit, and poisons life," Edson said of these years. "Poverty, in short, is being robbed of self-respect and self-reliance. Poverty is fear."[7]

To help support his family, Edson began working at the age of seven. He shined shoes for fans at the BAC soccer stadium and for travelers passing through the Baurú railroad station. He also stole peanuts from freight trains in the railroad yard and sold them outside the town's movie theater.

To help put food on the table, Edson sometimes went fishing in a stream that ran through his neighborhood. Since he did not own a fishing pole, he would wade out into the water, hold a mesh screen in the current, and scoop up any fish that became caught in it.

Losing Interest in School

Edson's constant struggle against poverty made earning money and playing soccer—which had the potential to turn into a career—seem more important than school. Children in Brazil usually attend four years of primary school and four years of secondary school. This amount of education is roughly equivalent to attending elementary school, middle school, and two years of high school in a typical American school system.

Dreaming about Traveling the World

As a child, one of Pelé's favorite pastimes was to watch small planes taking off and landing at an airport near his family's home. Whenever he could not gather enough friends for a soccer game, he would sneak off to the Aero Club for the afternoon. As he watched the planes, he often dreamed of climbing into one, flying through the sky, and looking down upon his house and town. This dream provided Pelé with an imaginary escape from the poverty and hardship he faced in his youth.

Although Edson was a bright boy, he found it hard to sit still and pay attention in class. "I would play a lot of hooky and go into the fields and practice soccer," he recalled. "I just didn't like the rigors of education. I didn't like being forced to sit in class and listen to the teacher."[8]

Edson's worst school experience came in his third year of primary school. He had a very strict teacher who used a variety of cruel punishments to keep order in the classroom. Whenever Edson talked in class, for example, the teacher stuffed crumpled paper into his mouth and made him hold it until his cheeks ached. When he misbehaved in other ways, the teacher spread small, hard beans on the floor and forced Edson to kneel on top of them. This teacher's harsh punishments added to Edson's dislike for school.

After completing the fourth year of primary school, Edson dropped out. He actually had six years of education by this time, because he had been forced to repeat both the third and fourth years of primary school because of poor attendance. After quitting school, Edson took a job at a boot factory making the equivalent of two dollars per day. Edson gave most of this money to his parents to help support the family.

The Shoeless Ones

As Edson's interest in school faded, soccer took on even greater importance in his life. When he was around ten years old, Edson and some of his school friends formed a soccer team. Since all the boys were too poor to afford shoes, they played barefoot and called their team the Shoeless Ones. They spent every spare minute of their time practicing—often skipping school to play soccer—and soon became a very good team. The Shoeless Ones also managed to find a real soccer ball. Although the ball was worn out and lopsided, it worked much better than an old sock stuffed with rags.

The Shoeless Ones played in the streets or in vacant lots against teams of boys from nearby neighborhoods. Most of their opponents played barefoot too. Without referees or proper equipment, the games tended to be very rough. Many boys ended up pushing, kicking, or tackling to try to steal the ball from the other team.

"You could say that they often got out of hand," Edson's brother, Zoca, said of the barefoot soccer games.

> A player would try to take the ball away from my brother and my brother would make him look silly, so he would turn around and hit my brother and my brother would come right back and take a swing at the kid who hit him. Often the games were broken off when everyone got involved in fights.[9]

The rough-and-tumble game of barefoot soccer helped Edson improve his skills. He developed creative ways of handling the ball in order to avoid contact with his opponents. He also became a tough player who could score goals even when another player fouled him. Over time, many people in Brazil began to link Edson's athletic style of play with barefoot soccer. In fact, after Edson became famous as Pelé, the game of barefoot soccer became known as pelada.

Receiving a Nickname

As Edson's soccer talents grew, his friends gave him the nickname Pelé. Many of the top soccer players in South America, like his father Dondinho, are known by one-word nicknames. Some people believe that this tradition started with radio announcers, who often shortened players' names to make it easier to describe fast-paced soccer games on radio broadcasts. Still, Edson was angry when his friends started calling him Pelé. "I have no idea where the name came from, or who started it," he said. "It has no meaning in Portuguese—or any other language, as far as I know."[10]

One of Edson's boyhood friends suggested that the nickname Pelé might have come from the way Edson pronounced Bilé, the name of a famous Brazilian goalkeeper. Another friend thought he remembered hearing the word shouted by Turkish immigrants who lived near the soccer field in Baurú. In any case, because the origins of the name were unclear, Edson believed it must be an insult. He often got into fights with boys who called him Pelé. Edson did not like the name, but it soon stuck, and he eventually came to accept it.

Learning from His Father

When it became clear that Pelé had great natural ability, his father began teaching him some of the finer points of soccer. Dondinho showed him the proper technique for striking the ball with his head. The former star also taught his son how to kick the ball equally well with both feet in order to keep opponents off balance.

In addition to these physical skills, Dondinho shared a number of other tips that helped make Pelé a better player. For instance, Dondinho taught Pelé to remain calm and focused during a game, even if an opponent fouled or taunted him. He explained that opposing players wanted him to lose his temper because it made him less effective on the field. Dondinho also shared his views of being a good sport and a team player.

Finally, Dondinho set a good example for Pelé by taking care of his health and avoiding cigarettes and alcohol. These lessons helped Pelé understand the dedication it took to become a top athlete. "I, who didn't listen to many people, listened to him because I thought—and still think—that Dondinho was one of the best players in Brazil, even if an injury kept him from ever reaching the top," he explained. "And I also listened because I knew he loved me and was trying to help me. Dondinho was a marvelous teacher."[11]

Star of the Bauru Junior Tournament

When Pelé was twelve years old, he got an exciting opportunity to show off the skills he had learned from his father. The mayor of Baurú decided to hold a soccer tournament for local boys' teams at the BAC Stadium, and the Shoeless Ones were invited to take part. In order to play in the tournament, though, the teams had to wear shoes. Luckily for Pelé and his friends, the father of three boys who played for the Shoeless Ones was a very good salesman. He persuaded a local men's soccer team to donate their old, worn-out shoes for the boys to wear in the tournament. Since they no longer played barefoot, the Shoeless Ones changed the name of their team to Amériquinha (Little America).

It took some time for Pelé and his teammates to get used to wearing shoes and playing on a proper soccer field. "Having played on streets full of potholes and on fields that were either uphill or downhill but never flat, and having played without football shoes using a ball made with rags stuffed into a sock—well, playing with proper equipment on proper grass was as close to heaven as any of us ever thought we'd get," he recalled. "And our play improved accordingly."[12]

Led by Pelé, Amériquinha did very well in the Baurú junior tournament. During the final game, Pelé dazzled the crowd with his speed, movements, ball-handling skills, and scoring ability. When he heard the 5,000 spectators at BAC Stadium chanting "Pelé! Pelé! Pelé!," he finally started to accept his nickname. After the match ended, Amériquinha received a trophy from the mayor, and Pelé was honored as the top scorer of the tournament. Pelé felt especially proud when Dondinho congratulated him on the victory and told him that he had played the game perfectly.

Getting Discovered

Pelé's performance in the Baurú junior soccer tournament brought him a great deal of attention. People all around Baurú told stories about the young player who had amazed the crowd with his athletic ability. One of the people who heard these stories was Waldemar de Brito, a former star who had played for Brazil in the 1934 World Cup tournament.

Great Talent

"I couldn't believe that such a young boy was able to perform some of the moves as well as the tricks with the ball that Pelé was doing," Coach Waldemar de Brito recalled. "I knew then that this boy had great talent."

Waldemar de Brito, quoted in Joe Marcus, *The World of Pelé*. New York: Mason/ Charter, 1976.

De Brito coached a men's soccer team at the Baurú Athletic Club. He soon persuaded the club's owners to sponsor a youth soccer team. He explained that a youth program could help develop a group of young, talented players who might eventually join the men's team. De Brito decided that he wanted to see Pelé play in person. If the boy was as good as people said, de Brito felt that he would be an ideal player to build a youth team around.

The coach found Pelé playing against a group of older construction workers on their lunch break. As de Brito watched, Pelé used an endless variety of moves to score goal after goal against the larger, stronger men. Recognizing his potential, de Brito invited the boy to join the Baurú Athletic Club's new youth soccer team, which was called Baquinho, or Little BAC.

Pelé eagerly accepted the opportunity to play for Baquinho and train under the well-known coach. He recalled the day he received his first real soccer uniform as one of the most thrilling moments of his life. "I took the uniform home to show my parents," he said. "When I saw how proud my father was, I cried."[13]

Working Hard

For the next three years, de Brito worked with Pelé one-on-one and also served as the coach of the Baquinho junior team. De Brito treated the boys the same way that he treated his adult

The bicycle kick became Pelé's most famous move, and many other players copied it.

players. He expected them to behave both on and off the field, and he taught them to play with discipline as a team. Pelé recognized the value of de Brito's knowledge and worked hard to apply all of the coach's suggestions. He often arrived at practice earlier than, and stayed later than, his teammates in order to work on specific skills. Sometimes Pelé was so exhausted by the time he got home that he went straight to bed without even eating dinner.

Although Pelé's natural position was center-forward, de Brito asked him to play every position on the field in order to develop a variety of skills. The coach also taught Pelé to keep track of all the action on the field so that he could react instantly when he received a pass. In addition, de Brito taught Pelé his most famous move: the bicycle kick. To do a bicycle kick on a ball in mid-air, a player jumps into the air and positions his body horizontally, with one knee bent. Then he extends the leg and kicks the ball backward, over his head, and lands on his back on the ground. Pelé became so good at the bicycle kick that many soccer fans think he invented the move.

Making Soccer a Career

De Brito's training helped Pelé become a star of the Brazilian youth soccer league. During the 1954 season, for example, he scored 148 goals in thirty-three games. He led Baquinho to Brazil's junior soccer championship three years in a row.

Many Skills
An average-sized man, he was blessed with speed, great balance, tremendous vision, the ability to control the ball superbly, and the ability to shoot powerfully and accurately with either foot and with his head.

"Pelé Biography," available online at http://www.360soccer.com/pele/pelebio.html.

After Baquinho won its third title in 1955, de Brito decided that his star player was ready to turn professional. In early 1956, the coach met with Pelé's parents and persuaded them to allow their fifteen-year-old son to try out for Santos, a top team in Brazil's professional soccer league. Although his mother worried that Pelé was too young to leave home, his father encouraged him to take advantage of the opportunity.

In June 1956, Pelé and his coach boarded a train in Baurú to travel to Santos. Dozens of Pelé's friends, family members, former teammates, and co-workers from the shoe factory gathered at the train station to see him off. For Pelé, the journey marked the beginning of a long and successful career in soccer.

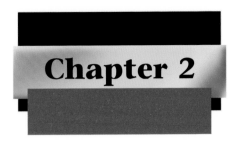

Chapter 2

Teenage Sensation Wins First World Cup

Pelé started his professional soccer career in Santos in June 1956. When he first arrived in the seaside town, he was a lonely, homesick fifteen-year-old boy. Pelé worked hard, stayed out of trouble, and grew up quickly. Less than two years later, the teenager became a national hero by leading Brazil's soccer team to its first World Cup championship.

Trying Out for Santos

When Pelé traveled from his hometown of Baurú in central Brazil to the coastal town of Santos in 1956, it was the first time he had ever been on a train. He felt scared and sick for much of the journey, but he still managed to enjoy his first glimpse of the Atlantic Ocean.

As soon as Pelé reached Santos, his coach, Waldemar de Brito, took him to meet the directors of the Santos professional soccer team. Even though Pelé was a skinny fifteen-year-old boy at the time, de Brito told the team officials that he would become the greatest soccer player in the world someday. Of course, the Santos directors had heard such bold claims from many coaches before.

They had great respect for de Brito, however, so they agreed to let Pelé try out for the team.

When Pelé went out onto the field for his tryout, he was surprised to receive a friendly greeting from the Santos players. "I could hardly believe I was actually there, meeting and shaking hands with the famous names I had only known from football cards or from hearing their names on the radio or reading of them in the *Baurú Daily*," he remembered. "It was an odd feeling, as if I might wake up at any minute and find myself in my bed at home, dreaming."[14]

At first Pelé felt very nervous, but he calmed down once he started kicking the ball around. He impressed the Santos coaches and players with his speed, movements, and ball-handling skills. After the tryout ended, the team directors recognized that Pelé had the potential to play professional soccer. Because of his small size, however, they decided to let him join the Santos juvenile team, which was for young players between the ages of fifteen and eighteen.

Working His Way Up

Upon joining the Santos development program, Pelé received free food and lodging and a few dollars in salary each month. Living on his own in a strange town often left him feeling lonely, scared, and homesick. Pelé fought to overcome these feelings by working hard and listening to his coaches. He also ate huge meals of high-protein foods in order to gain weight and increase his chances of making the Santos professional team.

Like many young players, Pelé spent the first few weeks with his new team practicing hard and sitting on the bench during games. He made his first appearance with the Santos juvenile team during a difficult match to decide the league championship. With the score tied at the end of the game, the coaches sent Pelé in to make a penalty kick. Facing only the opposing goalkeeper, with a chance to win the game, Pelé missed the shot. He felt so angry and embarrassed afterward that he packed up his suitcase to go back home. But luckily for him, a team official found out about his plan and persuaded Pelé to stay in Santos and continue practicing.

Although Pelé started on the Santos juvenile team, he was soon promoted to the professional team.

Within a few weeks, Pelé's hard work began to pay off. The Santos directors were so impressed by his ball control and passing abilities that they promoted him to the professional team. Pelé made his first professional soccer appearance on September 7, 1956, during an exhibition game against the Corinthians team from Santo André. After entering the game as a substitute in the second half, Pelé scored his first professional goal within a few minutes. He went on to play in ten more games that season, and he scored one more goal. In addition to its other rewards, becoming a professional soccer player helped Pelé to earn about $60 per month, most of which he sent home to his family.

By the start of his second professional season in 1957, Pelé joined the starting lineup for Santos. Although he was still smaller than the other players, Pelé worked so hard on his fitness that he could run faster and jump higher than many of them. He also showed a remarkable ability to score goals from anywhere on the field. In fact, he led the Brazilian professional league by scoring fifty-seven goals that season. Whenever opposing teams sent extra defenders to try to stop him from scoring, Pelé simply took advantage of the situation to pass the ball to an open teammate.

Joining the Brazilian National Team

As Pelé became one of the top players in the professional soccer league, some people wondered whether he might be selected to play for the Brazilian National Team. This elite, 22-member squad represented the country in international soccer competitions, including the upcoming 1958 World Cup tournament.

Players are chosen for this national team through a complicated process. Santos and other teams in the country's top leagues keep detailed records on every player. These records include game statistics as well as reports on the players' behavior and personalities. Each team is required to send its player records to Brazil's national soccer association. A group of association members known as the selection committee evaluates all of the top players to make sure that they are suitable to represent the country. Then the committee tries to put together a team with the strongest possible combination of skills.

Pelé wasn't yet 17 when he was chosen for the Brazilian National Team.

Many Santos fans hoped that Pelé would make the national team. They enjoyed watching the young player and felt that he would bring a great deal of energy and excitement to Brazil's squad. But some members of the selection committee had doubts about Pelé's youth, small size, and lack of experience in international competition.

Although playing for the Brazilian National Team was a life-long dream for Pelé, he tried not to get his hopes up before the selections were announced. "I told myself that if I didn't get picked on the squad, sure, I would be disappointed—but I also felt that I still had many years ahead of me for the chance,"[15] he said.

However, in June 1957 many people's faith was restored in Pelé when he played in his first international match. Pelé joined a group of stars from Santos and another top Brazilian team, Vasco da Gama, for an exhibition match against Belenenses, a popular team from Portugal that was touring South America. The match drew a huge crowd, and sixteen-year-old Pelé gave the audience much to cheer about. He scored three goals to help lift the Brazilian team to a 6–1 victory over their rivals.

A short time later, the selection committee announced that Pelé would be a member of the Brazilian National Team. He heard the news on the radio during a visit to his parents' house in Baurú. Once he got over the initial shock, Pelé cried tears of joy at having an opportunity to play for his country.

Facing International Competition

Shortly after his selection was announced, Pelé started playing with the national team. He scored his first goal for Brazil on July 9, 1957, three months before he turned seventeen. Pelé entered a game against Argentina in the second half and scored Brazil's only goal in a 2–1 loss. A few days later, when the two nations met again, Pelé started the game for Brazil. The teenager played brilliantly—using his speed and agility to dribble around much larger and more experienced defenders—and scored a goal to help Brazil claim a 2–0 victory.

While Pelé won over many Brazilian soccer fans with his strong play, some people still did not like the fact that a teenager had been chosen to represent the country. They blamed Pelé whenever the national team performed poorly. In an exhibition match against Juventus of Italy, for example, Pelé missed a couple of good scoring chances, and the crowd complained about it with a chorus of boos. When Pelé finally broke through the Italian defense for a beautiful goal, he rushed toward the stands and punched his fist in the air in triumph. From this time on, Pelé punched the air in salute whenever he scored a goal.

In April 1958, Pelé left Santos to train full-time with the Brazilian National Team in preparation for the World Cup. This important competition is held every four years to find the best soccer team in the world. Fifty-three nations applied to compete in the opening stages of the 1958 tournament. These countries played each other in a series of qualifying tournaments to decide the final sixteen teams that would compete for the World Cup. The field included the fourteen teams that performed best in the qualifying rounds, as well as the host country (Sweden) and the defending World Cup champion (West Germany). The sixteen teams were then divided into four groups. Each team in the group played the other three teams, and the two teams with the best records from each group went forward to the final stages.

Despite its great soccer tradition, Brazil had never won the World Cup tournament. In fact, the country had only reached the finals once, in 1950. Although Brazil hosted the tournament that year and was thought to be a favorite, the nation suffered a heartbreaking defeat to Uruguay. Brazilian soccer fans desperately wanted the 1958 team to erase these bad memories.

Playing for the World Cup

Despite the fans' high hopes for the team, most experts gave Brazil only a slight chance of winning the 1958 World Cup. Nevertheless, Pelé and his teammates believed that they had the talent to claim the ultimate prize in world soccer. Brazil had a

The Brazilian National Team carries the Brazilian flag around the stadium.

tough goalkeeper in Gilmar, and a quick, punishing offensive attack featuring Garrincha, Vavá, Mazzola, and Zagalo. The team also had a secret weapon in Pelé, who was relatively unknown in international soccer.

At seventeen, Pelé was the youngest player ever to appear in the World Cup tournament at that time. When he made the trip to Sweden for the competition, it was the first time Pelé had ever traveled outside of Brazil. Many of his Brazilian fans worried that the young, inexperienced player would struggle under the intense pressure of the competition.

Brazil was forced to play its first two group matches without Pelé, who suffered a knee injury in a warm-up match. Pelé watched from the bench as his teammates defeated Austria 3–0 and struggled to a 0–0 tie with England. Brazil then faced the Soviet Union, a powerful team that many people thought was the favorite to win the tournament. Knowing that the team needed a victory to advance to the finals, the Brazilian coaches asked Pelé to play despite his injury.

As Pelé and his teammates took the field for the all-important match, they noticed that the Soviet players were much bigger than the Brazilians. The Soviet goalkeeper, Iachine, was so huge that he made the goal seem tiny. Pelé was the smallest player on the field, and several reporters said he looked like a child compared to the Soviet squad. As soon as the game began, however, the speedy Brazilians ran circles around their opponents. Brazil controlled the ball well and prevented the Soviets from mounting an offensive attack. Pelé hit the goal post with a shot and helped to set up a teammate's goal as Brazil won the game, 2–0.

Getting the World's Attention

The victory over the Soviet Union meant that Brazil could go through to the quarterfinals of the World Cup tournament, where they faced Wales. After beating the powerful Soviet team, however, Pelé and his teammates grew overconfident. They underestimated the Welsh team and expected an easy warm-up for the semifinal round. Instead, the Brazilians found themselves deadlocked in a scoreless tie for most of the match. Welsh goalkeeper Jack Kelsey played brilliantly to stop Brazil's fast-paced scoring attack.

Finally, late in the second half, Pelé broke through the Welsh defenses and aimed a soft shot toward the goal. Kelsey was about to make the save when the ball hit a Welsh defender's foot and bounced past the keeper and into the goal. Pelé jumped into the air, then ran around in circles, and finally cried in relief. It was his first goal in a World Cup competition and the only goal of the match, as Brazil squeaked out a 1–0 victory. "That was certainly my most unforgettable goal—my luckiest, as has been said, possibly—but definitely my most unforgettable,"[16] he declared.

In the semifinals, Brazil faced France, which had scored more goals than any other team up to that point in the tournament. Brazil took the lead only two minutes into the game, with Pelé assisting on a goal by Vavá. But France came back to tie the game seven minutes later, scoring the first goal of the tournament against Brazilian goalkeeper Gilmar. Pelé refused to allow his teammates to lose their focus. "Pelé grabbed the ball out of the net and sprinted back upfield for the restart," a reporter recalled.

> There were still eighty-one minutes to play, and here was this teenager acting like a quarterback in a two-minute drill. 'Let's go! Let's get started! Let's quit wasting time!' he shouted, waving his elder teammates into position. They stared at him, and then, together, they scored the next four goals.[17]

Brazil took the lead 2–1 just before the end of the first half. When Pelé took the field for the second half, he found that the tired French defense left him room to move around. He responded by putting on a display that a veteran reporter described as "simply remarkable."[18] Pelé dribbled around the French defenders and scored two quick goals. When the defenders managed to surround him, he made a perfect pass to one of his teammates.

Pelé scored his third goal of the match with a trick known as a hat or sombrero play. He kicked the ball just over the head of an approaching defender, quickly moved around the opposing player, and kicked the ball into the net before it had even hit the ground. France managed to score another goal shortly before the final whistle, but the outcome of the game had already been decided, with Brazil claiming a 5–2 victory. After his amazing three-goal

In the 1958 World Cup semifinal match against France, Pelé scored three goals.

performance, Pelé found himself surrounded by reporters from all over the world. He found the attention a bit overwhelming, but he knew that his family and friends back home would be very excited to hear that he had done well.

Winning the Cup for Brazil

Pelé and his teammates had only a few days to enjoy the victory before they faced Sweden in the World Cup finals, which took place on June 29, 1958. The host country had earned a spot in the finals with a dramatic 3–1 semifinal win over defending champion West Germany. More than 60,000 Swedish fans crammed into the stadium to cheer their team on, many of them wearing the Swedish colors and carrying a wide assortment of noisemakers.

Although the hometown crowd favored Sweden, Pelé felt optimistic about his team's chances of winning Brazil's first World Cup title. "We had several things on our side," he noted.

We had a brand of football that combined great team play with the best of individual talent; and we also had our driving ambition to take the World Cup back to Brazil, which we, at least, were sure was greater than anyone else's ambition.[19]

The finals began on a note that tested Pelé's confidence. Sweden scored a goal only four minutes into the match, putting Brazil behind for the first time in the tournament. Pelé and his teammates remained calm, however, and quickly launched their offensive attack. A writer for the official Fédération Internationale de Football Association (FIFA) World Cup Web site said that Pelé "was unstoppable, [combining] perfect technique with lightning

Pelé was hugged by his fellow team members when he scored the winning goal.

speed, opportunism, and intelligence."[20] The Brazilians soon took control of the game with two goals by Vavá, one by Zagalo, and two by Pelé.

One of the goals that Pelé scored is often mentioned to be among the most spectacular scores in tournament history. Facing away from the Swedish goal, he caught a long pass with his chest, transferred the ball to his left foot, flipped it up over his shoulder, spun around, and kicked it into the net without ever letting it hit the ground. Even the Swedish goalkeeper, Svensson, cheered after the play. "I have never seen anything like that before and I doubt if I will ever see a goal scored like that again," he stated. "It was unbelievable."[21]

When the game ended in a 5–2 victory for Brazil, Pelé was so overwhelmed with emotion that he nearly fainted on the field. His teammates ran over and helped him up, then they lifted him onto their shoulders and carried him around the stadium. An article that appeared in the *New York Times* the following day

Pelé scored a spectacular goal in the final against Sweden.

noted that "the Brazilians dominated the Swedes in every respect. Their dribbling, surprising changes of pace and direction, and their quick-witted passing game often made the Swedes look like schoolboys."[22]

The One and Only

Such was his greatness that whenever Brazil are mentioned, the name that comes first to football fans' lips everywhere is Pelé... the one and only.

"Pelé," *The International Football Hall of Fame*, 2000. Available online at http://www.ihof.com/hof/pele.asp.

With six goals in the last three World Cup matches, Pelé had played an important role in bringing Brazil its first world championship. Upon returning home to Brazil, he and his teammates were greeted as national heroes. More than 5,000 fans met them at the airport in Rio de Janeiro, and hundreds of thousands more turned out when they were honored with a parade and fireworks.

Enjoying a Great Year

Winning the World Cup title in 1958 turned out to be just the start of an incredible year for Pelé. Between Santos and the Brazilian National Team, he scored a total of eighty-seven goals that year. His strong performance made him a favorite choice as Brazil's top soccer player of the year. Pelé received a salary increase from Santos as well as a number of performance bonuses. He was delighted to use the money to pay off the loan on his parents' house in Baurú and to pay travel expenses for family members to visit him in Santos.

Another important event occurred that year when Pelé met Rosemeri dos Reis Cholby, his future wife. They met on a rainy day when Pelé and a few of his teammates decided to drop in on a girls' basketball game. Pelé noticed Rosemeri sitting on the bench and was struck by her beauty. He spoke to her briefly after the game and learned that she worked in a record shop. Pelé started visiting Rosemeri at the shop, and they soon began dating. In order to

Setting a Good Example

After starring for Brazil in the 1958 World Cup tournament, Pelé became a national hero and a huge celebrity. Even as he grew famous, however, he remained a humble, hardworking young man who was deeply dedicated to the game of soccer. He continued to practice hard to develop his skills, and he paid close attention to his diet and training program. Pelé also took the time to talk with, and sign autographs for, his many fans.

Pelé's fame brought him a number of endorsement opportunities. Even at a young age, though, Pelé was careful to promote only products that fit with his image and values. For this reason, he refused to advertise alcohol and tobacco products. "I know that I have influence on youngsters," he explained, "and I don't feel that I want them to think if I should endorse these products I want them to use them."

Even after he became a world-famous celebrity, Pelé took the time to sign autographs and talk with his many fans.

Pelé, quoted in Joe Marcus, *The World of Pelé*. New York: Mason/Charter, 1976.

protect her from the media attention that always followed him, Pelé dated Rosemeri secretly for several years. "I feel that meeting her was one of the greatest days of my life," he said, "even if she never got into the basketball game and just sat on the bench."[23]

Protecting a National Treasure

Pelé's relationship with Rosemeri bloomed at a time when his skills on the soccer field were in high demand. In 1959, shortly after he turned eighteen, Pelé started his compulsory year of service in the Brazilian Army. He played soccer for the army team and also continued to play for both Santos and the Brazilian National Team. Pelé set a record by scoring 127 goals that year. He thanked Coutinho, a Santos teammate for some of this achievement—Coutinho always seemed to give him great passes to set up goals.

In 1960, Pelé's goal total dropped to seventy-eight, largely because opponents chose to double-team him. Although this was a significant drop from the previous year's total, Pelé remained the top scorer in the Brazilian professional soccer leagues. But Pelé did not worry himself about individual statistics—he was just pleased that Santos won the league championship.

The following year Pelé scored 110 goals to lead Santos to a second league title in a row. He also reached a career milestone in having scored 400 goals by 1961, shortly before he turned twenty years old. By this time Pelé had grown so famous that people around the world would give anything for a chance to see him play. Santos received so many offers to play exhibition matches that the team's management had to turn most of them down.

As Pelé's fame spread around the world, a number of the top professional soccer teams in Europe tried to lure him away from Santos. In fact, Pelé received offers of more than a million dollars to play in Europe, at a time when no professional soccer player had yet earned more than $100,000 per year. According to international soccer rules, Pelé could still represent Brazil in the World Cup and other international competitions, even if he played professionally in another country.

A Myth

You didn't have to see him to believe in him. His name became a myth that traveled to the far reaches of the world. The world wanted to touch, to witness Pelé.

Gentry Kirby, "Pelé, King of Futebol," available online at http://www.espn.go.com/classic/biography/s/Pele.html.

Leaders in the Brazilian government knew that the nation's many soccer fans would be devastated if Pelé left the country. To prevent this from happening, President Janio Quadros officially

As one of the most popular athletes in the world, Pelé had his own post-age stamp.

The Goal of the Plaque

Pelé scored many memorable goals during his long career. One of the most famous came in March 1961, during a game between Santos and the Fluminense team from Rio de Janeiro. The bitter rivals faced off in front of a capacity crowd of 100,000 people at Maracaná Stadium in Brazil.

Pelé received a pass near midfield and dribbled the ball around, through, or past nearly every member of the Fluminense squad. Two more defenders came charging toward him as he neared the goal, and he gave them a fake that sent them crash-ing into each other. With only the Fluminense goalkeeper left to beat, Pelé waited for him to commit and then dribbled around him and right into the goal.

The huge crowd jumped to their feet and gave Pelé a standing ovation that lasted for ten minutes. The goal became so famous that a Brazilian newspaper put up a plaque at the entrance to Maracaná Stadium to commemorate it. Ever since then, Pelé's remarkable scoring effort against Fluminense has been known as the "goal of the plaque."

declared Pelé a "national treasure" and said that his services could not be exported from Brazil. Pelé felt deep loyalty toward Santos, the team that had given him his first real opportunity to make soccer a career. He never really planned to leave Brazil. In fact, at one point Pelé held a press conference and told the news media that he wanted to play the rest of his career for Santos. But still, Pelé continued to receive offers from foreign teams. One soccer club in Italy even threatened to file a lawsuit in international court to force Brazil to release the soccer star. The rumors and contro-versy made it clear that Pelé had become one of the most popular athletes in the world.

Chapter 3

Sidelined by Rough Play

By the 1960s, Pelé had become famous around the world for his soccer skills. He enjoyed many parts of his fame, including the opportunities it gave him to travel, connect with fans, and earn lots of money. At the same time, though, Pelé learned that fame brought some negative things to his life. He faced very high expectations, for example, as fans wanted to see him score multiple goals and lead his team to victory in every match. Pelé also struggled to handle the constant media attention. Finally, Pelé became a target for fouls and harassment from opposing players who wanted to win at any cost. These issues led to his frustration and disappointment when he was forced to sit out most of the 1962 and 1966 World Cup tournaments because of injury.

Enjoying Fame and Fortune

By the time he reached the age of twenty, Pelé was widely thought to be the best soccer player in the world. His many fans referred to him as *Pérola Negra* (the Black Pearl), because he was so precious, or simply as *O Rei* (the King), because he ruled the soccer world.

Endorsements enabled Pelé to become a millionaire.

Pelé's popularity brought him a wide range of business opportunities. He became involved in construction projects and rubber manufacturing. He also appeared in advertisements for shoes, sports equipment, watches, bicycles, and a number of other products. With his outgoing personality, Pelé found himself in demand as a soccer analyst for Brazilian newspapers and radio stations. He even appeared in a few television series and movies.

Along with the salary and bonuses he earned playing soccer for Santos and the Brazilian National Team, Pelé's marketing and business projects helped him to become a millionaire. He invested most of his money and continued to live a modest lifestyle, although he did sometimes enjoy sailing boats to take his friends and family deep-sea fishing.

Facing High Expectations

Pelé's busy schedule did not allow him much time to go fishing or manage his business projects, especially when the 1962 World Cup tournament was around the corner. He and his teammates faced very high expectations from soccer fans, many of whom believed that Brazil would successfully defend its title. After all, the tournament was being held in neighboring Chile, so the Brazilian team would get lots of support from South American fans. In addition, Brazil was automatically given a place in the sixteen-team final round as the defending champion. This allowed the team to plan its own training schedule instead of being forced to play a grueling series of qualifying matches. Finally, Brazil had a very strong team led by Pelé, the best player in the world.

Pelé and his teammates did not pay attention to people who said they would win the World Cup tournament easily. Instead, they practiced hard to improve their skills, their fitness, and their teamwork. During one of these practice sessions, Pelé felt some tenderness in his groin—the area where the muscles of the lower abdomen connect to the muscles of the upper thigh. He ignored the pain and continued training for the World Cup.

Thousands of Brazilian fans made the trip to Chile in May 1962 to watch the national team play the opening match of the tournament against Mexico. Pelé thrilled the crowd by setting up a teammate's goal and then beating four Mexican defenders to score a goal of his own. Thanks to his efforts, Brazil won the game 2–0.

Brazil faced Czechoslovakia in the second match of the 1962 World Cup tournament. Most fans expected the high-powered Brazilian attack to dominate the Czech squad. Early in the contest, however, Pelé made a hard kick and then collapsed onto the ground in pain. He suffered a tear in the groin muscle that had been bothering him for weeks. Although he remained on the field for the remainder of the match, Pelé could barely walk or kick the ball. The Brazilian team seemed lost without its star and struggled to a 0–0 tie.

Watching from the Sidelines

The injury prevented Pelé from playing in Brazil's third match, against Spain. Missing out on the action made Pelé feel frustrated and disappointed, as if he had let his fans and teammates down.

> How was it, I thought bitterly, that I could play between eighty and a hundred games a year for Santos, or for the army, or even for the Selection, and never miss a game—and every time a World Cup match came along, there I was on the sidelines?[24]

Many Brazilian fans worried that the national team could not win the World Cup without its biggest star. They were crushed when Spain came out strong and took an early 1–0 lead in the game. Fortunately for Brazil, Pelé's substitute, Amarildo, scored two goals in the second half to give the team a 2–1 victory.

Brazil went through to the quarterfinals, where it faced a strong team from England. Led by the speedy Garrincha (Little Bird), however, the Brazilians posted a 3–1 victory. Next came a rough semifinal match against Chile. Pelé and his teammates felt that the referees ignored a number of fouls by players from the host country. Nevertheless, Brazil earned a 4–2 victory after two goals from Garrincha and two from Vavá.

Pelé desperately wanted to play in the World Cup final, which featured a rematch between Brazil and Czechoslovakia. He felt much better in the days leading up to the match, so he told his coaches that he would be ready. Sadly, Pelé re-injured himself in practice just before the final match began. He was forced to watch from the sidelines as his teammates beat Czechoslovakia 3–1 to claim Brazil's second straight World Cup title. "I am disappointed that I was unable to play most of the games," he said afterward, "but thank God that Brazil won."[25]

Regaining His Form

It took Pelé two months to recover fully from his groin injury. Once he got back into action, however, he played as brilliantly as ever. He scored thirty-seven goals in twenty-six games to lead

In 1963, Pelé scored his 600th goal—and he was only twenty-three years old.

Santos to another title in the Brazilian professional league. As the top soccer club in Brazil, Santos earned a chance to compete for the Copa Libertadores, awarded to the best team in South America. Santos claimed the championship on the strength of Pelé's four goals in the four-game tournament.

The victory earned Santos a spot in the Copa Internationale, a best-of-three-match tournament between the top two professional soccer teams in the world. Pelé scored one goal in the first match and three in the second to lead Santos to a sweep over Benfica of Portugal for the World Club Championship. The Brazilian media recognized his strong performance by voting him the nation's player of the year.

Pelé's excellent play continued in 1963. He scored seventy-six goals that year, including the 600th of his career. Pelé led Santos back to the Copa Internationale, where they defeated AC Milan of Italy to earn a second straight World Club Championship. Pelé was the centerpiece of the Santos team's aggressive, ball-control offense. He broke through the Italian defense to score five goals in two games.

Enduring Rough Treatment

By 1964, many teams were working on their defensive strategies to try to stop Pelé. A number of teams played six men back on defense, rather than the usual four, in an effort to keep the Brazilian star away from the goal. Many opposing teams played roughly and committed fouls to prevent Pelé from scoring. It seemed that some of this harsh treatment was even meant to injure Pelé.

Pelé complained that this play was unsportsmanlike and made the game less exciting for fans. He was determined to ignore the harassment and continue playing his best. "There are too many opposing players I have encountered who because they don't have the skill try and make a big name for themselves by being known as the man who chopped Pelé down," he acknowledged. "This really sickens me and makes me play even harder, as they soon find out."[26]

The tougher defenses held Pelé to sixty goals in 1964. An incredible eight of these goals came in a single game between Santos

Pelé's Natural Advantages

Throughout his soccer career, Pelé trained hard to maintain his physical condition and improve his skills. Aside from his hard work, however, Pelé also had some natural advantages that helped him become the best soccer player in the world. In the mid-1960s, he took part in a series of medical tests to identify some of his physical gifts. These tests showed that Pelé's peripheral or side vision was 25 percent better than that of an average athlete. This natural advantage allowed him to see more of the action on the field than most other players. The tests also showed that Pelé had extremely quick reflexes that allowed him to react to changing situations a half-second faster than an average athlete. He made good use of this ability in the fast-paced game of soccer.

and Botofoga of Rio de Janeiro. Pelé's effort helped his team achieve the most lopsided victory in Brazilian professional soccer history—11–0.

In 1965, Santos hired a new trainer, Julio Mazzei, who used scientific principles in the team's fitness program. Pelé said his work with Mazzei helped him to increase his goal total to 101 that year.

Personal Highs and Lows

Pelé experienced some ups and downs in his personal life as well as in his career during the mid-1960s. On the positive side, Pelé became a homeowner for the first time. One of the directors of the Santos team had a house available in a nice neighborhood, just a few blocks from the beach. When Pelé worked out a new contract with Santos, he arranged for the house to be included in the deal. Since the kitchen of his new home was as large as his family's entire house in Baurú, he persuaded his parents and brother and sister to come live with him. He enjoyed coming home to a busy house full of relatives who cared for him.

Unfortunately for Pelé, he also discovered that some of his investments and business projects had been handled poorly. The young star kept so busy training, traveling, and playing soccer that he never paid much attention to his finances. Instead, he trusted a friend to manage his business interests. When several construction and manufacturing projects ran into problems, the friend did not tell Pelé until it was too late. By the time Pelé hired a financial expert to look into the situation, he had lost nearly all of his money and faced large debts. Determined to avoid bankruptcy, Pelé got a loan from the Santos directors and spent the next three years paying it back out of his salary.

Pelé's personal life started to look brighter again in February 1966, when he finally married his longtime girlfriend, Rosemeri dos Reis Cholby. As soon as Pelé announced his engagement, it became one of the biggest news stories in Brazil. The newspapers

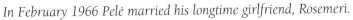

In February 1966 Pelé married his longtime girlfriend, Rosemeri.

were full of rumors and gossip in advance of the event. One source even claimed that Pelé would be married in the Maracaná Stadium in front of 100,000 people. Instead, Pelé and Rosemeri held a private wedding ceremony at home that was attended by a few close friends and relatives. In fact, the reporters outside Pelé's house greatly outnumbered the guests inside.

Pelé and his bride spent their honeymoon in Europe. Pelé remarked that it was the first time in his life that he had ever taken a vacation. The couple visited Paris, stayed at a castle in the Bavarian Alps, and toured Italy. They had the opportunity to meet a number of prominent people, including Pope Paul VI. Everywhere they went, soccer fans recognized Pelé and crowded around him, asking for autographs.

Trying for a Third World Cup

Shortly after Pelé returned from his honeymoon, he joined the Brazilian National Team to begin preparing for the 1966 World Cup tournament. If Brazil managed to become the first nation to win the title three times, it would take permanent possession of the Jules Rimet Trophy. Throughout the 36-year history of the World Cup, this trophy had always been presented to the tournament champion. But FIFA, the international soccer federation that ran the World Cup, planned to retire the trophy when the tournament got its first three-time winner.

Ideal Soccer

"I am not sad at defeat, only that I have not been allowed to play soccer," Pelé said following Brazil's devastating loss in the 1966 World Cup tournament. "Ideal soccer has become impossible. This is terrible for the game and for the spectators who want a show."

Pelé, quoted in "Rough Tactics in Cup Tourney Put World Soccer on Defensive," *New York Times*, July 25, 1966, p. 31.

Brazil had many strong players suitable for the national team, and many people believed that the Brazilians had a good chance of defending their World Cup championship. According to Pelé, however, Brazil's selection committee invited far too many players to try out for the national team. Then the coaches, who spent a lot of time fighting amongst themselves, divided all the players into groups and trained them separately. The top players did not get a chance to practice together as a team because they were usually training with different groups. In addition, the coaches waited a long time to make their choices, which left the players feeling nervous and uncertain about their situation. As a result of these problems, Pelé gradually lost confidence in the coaches and worried about the team's chances in World Cup competition. "There is only one way to describe Brazil's 1966 World Cup effort, and that is to openly declare that from beginning to end it was a total and unmitigated disaster,"[27] he recalled.

When the Brazilian team arrived in England to take part in the sixteen-team group round of the tournament, the defending champions found another problem. The European referees allowed the competitors to play in a very physical way. The officials called very few penalties, even when players kicked, tripped, and pushed one another. A reporter for the *New York Times* described such tactics, known as "padlock" or "blanket" defense, as "rough, often violent play, no-holds-barred attempts to keep opponents from entering the goal area at any cost."[28] This situation favored the European teams—which tended to be bigger, stronger, and better at defense—over smaller, quicker, and more aggressive teams like Brazil.

Playing in Pain

Brazil came across this style of defense in the opening match of the 1966 World Cup tournament, against Bulgaria. The Bulgarian defenders took full advantage of the slack referees and played a rough, physical game. Pelé was the main target of their abuse. One Bulgarian player, Zhechev, fouled the Brazilian star repeatedly throughout the game, twice knocking him down from behind. Many observers felt it was clear that Zhechev wanted to injure Pelé and force him out of the tournament. A French reporter, watching the action from the press box, commented that "Pelé won't finish the World Cup [under these circumstances]. It's amazing that he hasn't gone mad."[29] Still, the referees failed to call any fouls against Zhechev.

Despite the harsh treatment he received, Pelé managed to score a goal against Bulgaria, becoming the first player ever to score in three World Cup tournaments. Brazil won the game, 2–0, but Pelé felt so sore afterward that he was not sure whether he would be ready to play in the next round. Since the Brazilian team faced Hungary, which was considered to be one of the weaker teams in the tournament that year, Pelé's coaches decided to rest him and several other top players. This led to disaster, however, because Hungary gave Brazil its first loss in a dozen years of World Cup competition—3–1.

Feints and Footwork

"Frequently the victim of unscrupulous defenders, Pelé rarely retaliated," Jack Rollin wrote in *The World Cup, 1930–1990*. "He invariably humiliated his opponents with feints and footwork, achieving his own kind of retribution with consummate ease."

Jack Rollin, *The World Cup, 1930–1990*. New York: Facts on File, 1990, p. 135.

Following the loss to Hungary, Brazil faced a tough team from Portugal. Pelé and his teammates knew that they had to win the match to have any chance of getting to the quarterfinals. Although Pelé had not completely recovered from his injuries, he returned to action for this all-important game. Once again, he found himself the target of many violent collisions and tackles by the Portuguese defenders. At one point, an opposing player named Morais tripped Pelé. While Pelé was still lying on the ground, Morais stepped on his knee. Although Pelé was seriously injured, the English referee did not call a foul on the play. "It wasn't until I actually saw the films of the game that I realized what a terribly vicious double foul it was," Pelé said afterward. "Even in the most inexperienced league in the world, he would have been thrown out for either one."[30]

Brazil lost the game 3–1 and was out of the first round of the World Cup tournament for the first time since 1934. The nation went into mourning following the loss, and black flags flew across

Rio de Janeiro. England went on to beat West Germany in the World Cup finals, finishing a tournament that would long be remembered for its rough play and poor refereeing. Pelé felt so disgusted afterward that he vowed never again to play in World Cup competition.

Feeling Tired

Pelé's disappointment over the 1966 World Cup lasted for the rest of that year. As he struggled to regain his love for soccer, he scored only forty-two goals—the lowest total of his career. The main highlight of the season came when Pelé traveled to the United States for the first time to play a series of exhibition matches with his Santos team. Although soccer had not yet become popular in America, record crowds turned out to watch the great Pelé play against professional teams from around the

With his Santos team, Pelé played exhibition matches in the United States in 1968.

War Stops for Pelé

In 1968, Pelé traveled to Africa for the first time to play in a series of exhibition matches with his Santos team. African soccer fans were thrilled to have a chance to see him play, and he was greeted as a hero in many of the countries he visited. One of these countries was Nigeria, which was in the middle of a bloody civil war at the time Santos arrived in the [former] capital of Lagos. The people of Nigeria had such great interest in seeing Pelé play that both sides in the civil war agreed to stop fighting for two days. The match took place with tight security in front of the largest crowd ever to attend an African sporting event. No fighting occurred during this time, but the war started again the day after Pelé left the country.

Jack Rollin, *The World Cup*, 1930–1990. New York: Facts on File, 1990, p. 135.

world. The tour's success made Pelé think that soccer had the potential to take off in the United States.

Pelé's feelings of happiness over the successful U.S. tour continued into 1967. The year started out well for Pelé when his wife gave birth to their first child, a daughter named Kelly Christina. But the rest of the year was difficult for Pelé. The demands of practice and travel left him feeling physically tired, and he longed to spend more time at home with his family. Pelé raised his goal total to fifty-seven, but Santos slipped to the middle of the Brazilian professional league standings.

In 1968, both Pelé and his Santos team saw some improvement. Pelé scored a total of fifty-nine goals, including the 900th goal of his legendary career. He also enjoyed making another promotional tour of the United States with Santos. This time, Pelé and his teammates played a series of exhibition matches against teams from the newly organized North American Soccer League. These positive experiences helped Pelé to get back some of his passion for soccer. But he refused to consider representing Brazil in the upcoming 1970 World Cup tournament.

Chapter 4

Coming Back for Another World Cup Triumph

The 1966 World Cup tournament was a low point in Pelé's career. Opposing teams had fouled him so much that he was forced out of the competition with an injury. Without him, Brazil failed to defend its title. But it also failed to get through the group round of the competition. Pelé's anger and disappointment over the 1966 tournament were so strong that he declared he would not play for the Brazilian National Team in the 1970 World Cup.

Over time, however, a number of events persuaded Pelé to change his mind. In 1969, for example, he reached an impressive milestone by scoring the 1,000th goal of his legendary career. This achievement helped Pelé to regain his love for soccer and made him reconsider his decision about playing for the national team. Pelé played brilliantly in the 1970 World Cup and Brazil became the first nation to win a third title. After adding what he thought was the best achievement of his international soccer career, Pelé retired from the Brazilian National Team.

Reaching a Milestone

The frustration and disappointment that Pelé felt about the out-come of the 1966 World Cup tournament stayed with him for the next few years. Pelé wanted to avoid further injuries in rough international competitions, and he announced that his career with the Brazilian National Team was over. Instead, he focused his attention on playing for Santos in the Brazilian professional league and in an increasing number of exhibition matches around the world.

When Santos started its 1969 season, the Brazilian media noticed that Pelé was nearing the 1,000th goal of his career. Soccer fans across the country grew very excited about this approaching mile-stone. After all, it was unusual for any player to score more than 500 goals in his career, so many people thought that no one would ever reach 1,000 goals. "The 1,000 goal mark is a millennium in

An expectant crowd watched Pelé score his 1,000th goal in 1969.

soccer comparable to the four-minute mile or [American baseball player] Babe Ruth's sixty home runs in one season,"[31] explained a writer for the *New York Times*.

Weakness in Defense

The 1970 Brazilian World Cup team "readily admitted their weakness in defense. Their strength was in attack. They were there to score goals. If their defense gave one up, well, they would simply score two at the other end."

Paul Gardner, *The Simplest Game*. New York: Macmillan, 1996, p. xxi.

As the season went on, Pelé kept scoring goals and getting closer to the achievement. His goals received more and more attention in the press throughout South America. Soccer fans packed into stadiums whenever Santos played, in hopes of witnessing the big event. All of this anticipation made Pelé feel very nervous. The pressure affected his play as well as that of his team.

Pelé finally scored his 1,000th goal on November 19, 1969, during the 909th match of his career. The match saw Santos playing against league rival Vasco da Gama at Maracaná Stadium. Knowing that they might witness history, the crowd cheered wildly and waved flags and banners every time Pelé touched the ball. In the first half, he just missed the goal on two different shots, causing fans to groan in disappointment. Then an opposing player fouled Pelé, and the referee awarded him a penalty kick. He lined up twelve yards from the opposing goalkeeper, took some time to clear his head, then kicked the ball toward the net.

Once the ball went into the goal, Pelé trotted over, picked it up, and kissed it. He had time to shake hands with the opposing goalkeeper before being mobbed by his teammates. Thousands of fans rushed onto the field in celebration as fireworks went off around the stadium. Pelé's achievement secured his place as the best soccer player of all time. In fact, soccer fans across Brazil have celebrated the anniversary of the famous goal, known as *O Milésimo* (the thousandth), on November 19 every year since then.

Thousandth Goal

I would have been pleased to have been informed one morning that the day before I had scored the thousandth goal, but to have it ahead of me, and referred to daily in newspapers or on the radio, was unnerving.

Pelé, with Robert L. Fish, *My Life and the Beautiful Game: The Autobiography of Pelé*. Garden City, New York: Doubleday, 1977.

Changing His Mind

Pelé followed his 1,000th goal with four more that season, bringing his total to sixty-eight for the year. These goals helped Santos win the league championship for the third time in a row. More importantly, the historic season helped restore Pelé's love for soccer, and he began to reconsider his decision not to play for Brazil in the 1970 World Cup.

A number of other factors also influenced Pelé's feelings about rejoining the Brazilian National Team. First, he learned that the 1970 World Cup tournament would be played in Mexico. He believed that the fans, officials, and playing conditions in Mexico would favor Brazil over the European teams. Second, he found out that the tournament would be the first one ever broadcast around the world on color television. He came to view it as an important opportunity to promote soccer in the United States and other countries.

A third reason that Pelé reconsidered his decision was that the Brazilian media had finally started to recognize and discuss some of the problems that had contributed to the national team's failure in the 1966 World Cup tournament. Instead of placing the blame on Pelé and the other players, newspapers began to point out some of the mistakes made by the selection committee and coaches. Pelé felt sure that once these mistakes came out into the open, pressure from the Brazilian people would prevent the same thing from happening again in 1970.

Finally, Pelé liked and respected many of the players on the Brazilian National Team. Several of the best players from the 1966 squad—including the speedy Garrincha and goalkeeper Gilmar—had retired. But a number of talented young players had taken their places, including Rivelino, Jairzinho, and Tostão. Although Pelé still worried about being injured by the rough style of World Cup action, all of these factors combined to make him change his mind about playing in the 1970 tournament. Soccer fans across the country were thrilled when the 29-year-old veteran announced that he would come back to represent Brazil in the World Cup for a fourth time.

Coming Back Strong

Since Brazil had been knocked out early in the 1966 World Cup tournament, Pelé and his teammates had to play a series of six qualifying matches just to reach the group round of sixteen teams. With a fast-paced attack that often looked like a dance, Brazil easily got through the qualifying round. Pelé led the way with six goals in the six matches.

The Brazilian National Team arrived in Mexico three weeks before the World Cup tournament began. They spent this time getting used to the high altitude and intense heat in Mexico. They also managed to win over many Mexican soccer fans, especially around their practice area in Guadalajara, with their willingness to sign autographs and give interviews. By the time the Brazilians played their first match of the group round against Czechoslovakia, Pelé and his teammates had the crowd firmly on their side.

When the opening match began, the Brazilian squad seemed nervous. The Czechs took advantage of the situation to score an early goal. Within a short time, however, the Brazilian offensive attack came to life. Pelé and his teammates dominated the Czech defense with their ball control and won the match 4–1. The highlight of the match was a Pelé goal that amazed the crowd at the stadium and television viewers around the world. He received a pass from a teammate by trapping the ball with his chest, let it roll down to his foot, and then sent a booming kick into the net. And with that, Pelé became the first player ever to score a goal in four different World Cup tournaments.

A Classic Battle of Soccer Styles

Brazil's second match of the 1970 tournament is often mentioned among the classic World Cup games of all time. Pelé and his teammates faced England, the defending World Cup champion.

Hard feelings still existed between the two teams from the 1966 tournament. In addition, the two teams played very different styles of soccer. Unlike the aggressive "samba soccer" favored by Brazil, England played a tough, conservative, and defensive game. Many fans believed that the winner of the match would become the favorite to win the World Cup.

Brazil and England met on June 7 in the sweltering heat of Guadalajara. England tried hard to prevent Pelé from scoring. The English defender Alan Mullery followed Pelé wherever he went on the field, and they also put defender Brian Labrone in front of the goal to stop Pelé if he broke through.

Despite England's defensive measures, Pelé nearly scored an amazing goal in the first half. He jumped higher than several opponents and sent a sharp header toward the corner of the net. The shot appeared certain to go in when English goalkeeper Gordon Banks made one of the greatest saves in World Cup history. "As the ball screamed towards its destination inside the post, somehow, miraculously, Gordon Banks got a hand to it and flicked it up over the bar," recalled a writer for the International Football Hall of Fame Web site. "The save of the century? Probably. Pelé could only stand and stare in amazement—along with several million incredulous TV viewers around the world."[32]

The tense battle continued until Brazil's attack finally overcame the English defense. Pelé set up a goal by Jairzinho, giving Brazil a 1–0 victory. After the match ended, Pelé met England's captain, Bobby Moore, at midfield. To the delight of the crowd, the two players showed great sportsmanship by hugging each other and exchanging jerseys. In an interview following the game, Pelé also expressed his admiration for Gordon Banks. "He must be the greatest goalkeeper in the world. He got up like a cat. He made one of the best saves I have ever seen, and it was not his fault the English didn't win."[33]

Following the hard-fought victory over England, Brazil faced Romania in its third and final match of the group round. Needing only a tie against Romania, a team that many people viewed as one of the weakest in the tournament, Brazil decided to rest some of its stars. Pelé insisted on playing, however, and he scored two goals to lift his team to a 3–2 victory.

Helping His Teammates

The victory over Romania helped Brazil to win its group and advance to the quarterfinals of the World Cup tournament. In this match, Brazil faced a rival South American team, Peru. The coach of the Peruvian squad was Didi, a former star who had played alongside Pelé on Brazil's 1958 and 1962 World Cup champion teams. Many people thought Peru would be a tough opponent for Brazil because Didi was very familiar with the strengths and weaknesses of the Brazilian players.

To the surprise of Pelé and his teammates, Peru started out the match with an aggressive attack, similar to Brazil's famous style. But the Brazilian players used their superior ball control to take full advantage of the situation and easily won the match 4–2. Pelé helped to set up a goal by Tostão.

The victory allowed the Brazilians to advance to the semifinals, where they faced Uruguay. This match was the first time the powerful teams had met since the 1950 World Cup finals, which had been hosted by Brazil. Back in 1950, all of Brazil was ready to celebrate a victory. Instead, the team had suffered a heartbreaking defeat in front of their home crowd at Maracaná Stadium. "A football result has possibly never had such a strong and enduring impact on the emotional life of a nation," Alex Bellos wrote in *Futebol: Soccer, the Brazilian Way*. "The Maracaná Tragedy continues to morbidly fascinate Brazilians like no other event."[34] Even twenty years later, Brazil's soccer fans had not forgotten the devastating loss to Uruguay, and they desperately wanted Pelé and his teammates to take revenge.

Tensions about the game became even higher when Uruguay tried to change the location of the match. The Uruguayans recognized that fans in Guadalajara favored Brazil, so they argued that the game should be moved to Mexico City. Tournament officials did not agree, however, so the match took place as planned. From the opening whistle, Uruguay started to attack, hoping to beat Brazil at its own game. Some fans grew nervous when Uruguay took an early lead on a weak play by Brazilian goalkeeper Felix. Determined to keep his teammates' confidence up, Pelé immediately ran over and patted Felix on the back. The Brazilians followed his lead and soon took control of the game. Pelé helped to set up a goal by Rivelino, and Brazil secured a 3–1 victory.

Winning a Third World Cup

The triumph over Uruguay brought Brazil back to the World Cup finals, where the team faced Italy. Pelé felt very nervous as the game approached. "The pressure one feels in the final is many times the pressure one feels in any of the games leading up to the final," he explained. "The final is everything; it is for the championship. And the championship is all that counts. Second place may seem like a reasonable award to be proud of, but who remembers who placed second?"[35]

The final match of the 1970 tournament took place on June 21 at the modern Azteca Stadium in Mexico City. It was played in front of 112,000 spectators and a worldwide television audience estimated at 900 million people. Because both Brazil and Italy had won two previous World Cup titles, whichever team won the match would become the tournament's first three-time winner and would be allowed to keep the Jules Rimet Trophy.

As the match got underway, it became clear that Italy planned to concentrate on defense in order to stop Brazil's fast-moving attack. In fact, Italy sometimes kept as many as nine players back in its own end of the field to defend the ball. Although this style of play

Brazil won their third World Cup in 1970.

made it more difficult for the Italians to score, they hoped that their defensive play might force Brazil to give them the ball for a break-away opportunity.

Many people thought the Italian defense was unbeatable, but Pelé soon discovered a weakness. The veteran star received a high pass from Rivelino, leaped over several defenders, and headed the ball into the net for the opening goal of the match. It was the 100th goal ever scored by a Brazilian player in all of the nation's World Cup appearances.

Italy came back to tie the score before halftime, after capturing a wayward pass between the Brazilian goalkeeper and one of his defenders. In the second half, however, Pelé and his teammates increased the level of their play and dominated the Italian team. Pelé set up goals by Jairzinho and Carlos Alberto to lead Brazil to an impressive 4–1 victory. "The team played with such panache [style] that the final is generally regarded as the highest moment in Brazilian—if not world—football,"[36] Alex Bellos wrote in his book *Futebol: Soccer, the Brazilian Way*.

As soon as the match ended, thousands of cheering fans ran onto the field. They mobbed Pelé and the other Brazilian players, ripping off their clothing as souvenirs of the historic third championship. Left wearing only his underwear, an emotional Pelé was carried around the stadium on the shoulders of his fans. "This is the greatest excitement I have ever had as a player," he said afterward. "This championship gave me tremendous satisfaction and I enjoyed the competition. It was also the first time that I have been able to play an entire World Cup without getting injured."[37]

After the game, the Italian defender who played against Pelé, Tarcisio Burgnich, showed his admiration for Pelé's skills. "I told myself before the game, 'He's made of skin and bones just like everyone else'—but I was wrong,"[38] Burgnich stated. The *London Times* summed up Pelé's amazing performance with a headline the following day: "How do you spell Pelé? G-O-D."[39]

Changing His Focus

Brazilian soccer fans reacted with joy to the national team's World Cup triumph. Huge parties took place in Rio de Janeiro, São Paulo, and throughout the country. Thousands of people took to

Thousands of Brazilians celebrated the win with parades, parties, and fireworks.

the streets in celebration. They set off fireworks, drove around in specially decorated cars, or danced around carrying Brazilian flags or banners with pictures of their favorite players. The fans gave Pelé and his teammates a hero's welcome when they returned home to Brazil. They were honored with parties, parades, and meetings with the president and other important people.

Pelé enjoyed taking part in many of these events in the week following the World Cup victory. After awhile, though, Pelé began to grow tired of the hectic schedule and constant demands on his time. He longed to slow down and relax with his family, whom he had barely seen during the months when the national team was training for and competing in the World Cup tournament. When his wife Rosemeri—who was seven months pregnant with their second child at the time—asked him to come home, he decided to skip a team party in Sao Paulo to be with her. Unfortunately for Pelé, his decision disappointed many of his fans, and the Brazilian media criticized him for it.

On August 27, 1970, two months after his World Cup triumph, Pelé celebrated the birth of his son, Edson Cholby de Nascimento. "Now I had everything, a great wife, a wonderful daughter, and a son," he remembered. "It is really hard to describe your feelings at the minute you learn that you are the father of a son."[40]

Following the birth of his son, Pelé took some time off from soccer in order to focus his attention on his family. He and his wife worked together to design and oversee the construction of a new home in Santos, and by early 1971 it was ready for the family to move in. Although the three-story house had a simple design, it also included special features for each member of the family. For Rosemeri, who had a growing interest in photography, it included a darkroom. For Pelé, it included a room to hold the collection of trophies and memorabilia from his soccer career. The children got a swimming pool and a soccer practice area. Because of Pelé's fame, the house also had some necessary features to protect the family's privacy. A tall wall surrounded the house for example, and quarters were included for a security guard.

In addition to spending more time with his family, Pelé also became increasingly involved in managing his business interests. Pelé's promotion of various products and his investments in housing construction, rubber manufacturing, and port operations earned him more than one million dollars per year. He decided to set up offices to run these businesses in a building near his new home. His younger brother, Zoca, served as his lawyer and communications director. His good friend and former trainer, Mazzei, also came to work for him. Pelé understood that once his soccer career came to an end, he would need to concentrate on his business interests in order to support his family.

Going Out on Top

As Pelé gradually focused more on business and family, he began to think about retiring from the Brazilian National Team. He liked the idea of stepping down while he was at the peak of his career. Since he had recently played an injury-free World Cup tournament and led Brazil to a third title, the timing seemed right. Pelé also wanted to give the selection committee time to find and train his replacement. Pelé did not want to take a place on the

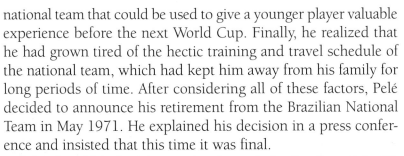

Rethinking Education

Around the time that Pelé retired from the Brazilian National Team, he also earned a college degree in physical education. This achievement took years of hard work. After all, Pelé had dropped out of primary school after completing only four grades. Before he could enroll in college, Pelé had to study for and pass both primary-school and secondary-school equivalency tests, as well as a university entrance exam. He spent a year preparing for each of these tests and another three years attending college. His friend and trainer Mazzei supported his efforts by giving him lectures and helping him study. Although it took a lot of time and hard work, Pelé felt that completing his college education was worth it. He knew that the degree would help him manage his business interests after his soccer career ended. He also believed that it would send a positive message about the importance of education to his children and his many young fans.

national team that could be used to give a younger player valuable experience before the next World Cup. Finally, he realized that he had grown tired of the hectic training and travel schedule of the national team, which had kept him away from his family for long periods of time. After considering all of these factors, Pelé decided to announce his retirement from the Brazilian National Team in May 1971. He explained his decision in a press conference and insisted that this time it was final.

Pelé played his final international match for Brazil on July 18, 1971. The Brazilian National Team played against Yugoslavia in front of 180,000 spectators in Rio de Janeiro. The special match, which organizers described as "Farewell to the King," was also broadcast worldwide on satellite television. As the game got underway, Pelé's many fans made it clear that they wanted to see him score one last goal. His teammates made every effort to create scoring opportunities for him. But Pelé remained a team player to the end, passing the ball to open teammates rather than forcing shots of his own. He did not get a goal in his final game for Brazil, which ended in a 2–2 tie.

The plan for Pelé's last game with the national team included a special ceremony at halftime. As the first half ended, Pelé jogged a lap around the field, waving his shirt in the air and acknowledging the standing ovation from the crowd. When he stopped in the center of the field, the spectators began chanting *"Fica! Fica!"* (Stay! Stay!). Pelé was so touched that tears began streaming down his cheeks. "It is all too overwhelming," he said. "I had tried to imagine what this would be like, but it surpassed anything I could think."[41] After the game ended, Pelé received messages of congratulations from a number of world leaders, including U.S. President Richard Nixon and England's Queen Elizabeth.

Pelé ended his remarkable career with the Brazilian National Team. His ninety-five goals in 111 game appearances put him in third

Wanting to go out on top, Pelé retired from the Brazilian National Team in 1971.

Promoting Soccer around the World

As Pelé prepared to end his career with the Brazilian National Team, he also began working to promote soccer around the world. He signed a contract with Pepsi-Cola, the international soft drink company, to launch the Pepsi International Soccer Program. The goal of the program was to teach soccer skills to young boys in 115 countries. During his travels with Santos and the national team, Pelé made personal appearances in many of these countries and gave soccer clinics for enthusiastic groups of young players. He also demonstrated various soccer techniques in an educational film series called *Pelé—The Master and His Method*. The films, which were distributed free of charge, became a huge success and won several international awards. Pelé felt extremely proud and grateful to have the opportunity to promote soccer to millions of children around the world.

Paul Gardener, *The Simplest Game*. New York: Macmillan, 1996, p. xxi.

place on the all-time list of goal scorers in international matches. Twelve of his career goals with the national team came during World Cup matches, which placed him fourth among all-time World Cup scorers, behind Ronaldo, Gerd Müller, and Just Fontaine.

With all the retirement festivities behind him, Pelé settled down to play out the remainder of his professional career with Santos. Although he still had to travel to play in international exhibition matches, most of his games took place in Brazil, and many of them were held at the local stadium in Santos. Pelé took advantage of this situation to spend more time with his family and to prepare for life after soccer.

Chapter 5

Bringing Soccer to America

Even after he retired from the Brazilian National Team in 1971, Pelé remained as big a star as ever. Fans packed into stadiums around the world to see him play for Santos over the next few years. As his playing days neared an end, Pelé became determined to use his popularity to promote the sport of soccer, especially in the United States.

Win a Country

"It really was ludicrous to think that Pelé, the greatest player of all, was going to end up playing for this ridiculous little team in New York," said Cosmos General Manager Clive Toye. "But I told him don't go to Italy, don't go to Spain, all you can do is win a championship. Come to the U.S. and you can win a country."

Quoted in Gentry Kirby, "Pelé, King of Futebol," available online at http://www.espn.go.com/classic/biography/s/Pele.html.

Shortly after he played his final game for Santos in 1974, Pelé shocked many people by coming out of retirement to play for

65

the New York Cosmos of the fledgling North American Soccer League. Although the Cosmos offered him a multimillion-dollar contract, Pelé claimed that his main goal was to create excitement about soccer among the American people. Pelé's involvement in the league led to a huge increase in crowd attendance and also encouraged young people to take part in youth soccer across the United States.

Playing Out His Career with Santos

Even after Pelé retired from the Brazilian National Team, he continued playing for Santos, the professional team that he had joined as a teenager. By this time—thanks to his brilliant performance in the 1970 World Cup tournament—Pelé was a national hero in Brazil and the best-known soccer player in the history of the game. Thousands of excited fans came to see Pelé wherever Santos played.

During the last few years of Pelé's playing career, team officials took advantage of his fame to turn Santos into one of the wealthiest sports franchises in the world. The club took large fees from dozens of other teams to play in international exhibition matches. Most of the contracts for these matches stated that the payment would be much smaller if Pelé failed to appear.

Pelé had hoped that playing only for Santos would allow him to spend more time with his family and focus on his growing business interests. He did not like the fact that Santos scheduled so many exhibition tours that required him to travel outside of Brazil. Pelé also felt disappointed that team officials did not use the time remaining before his retirement to find and train a young player to replace him. Instead, the Santos directors seemed more interested in using Pelé's name to make lots of money. Some Brazilian fans complained that Santos held its best players out of league games in order to save them for exhibition tours. In response, the Brazilian Soccer Federation threatened to force the team to cancel some of its foreign matches.

Sharing Skills

These issues and the team's hectic travel schedule, contributed to the fact that Pelé scored only thirty-four goals in 1971. The following year, however, Pelé began to change his view of the

One of Pelé's favorite experiences was giving soccer clinics to young players.

international exhibition matches. Santos made its first tour of Asia and Australia, and Pelé and his teammates took advantage of the opportunity to give soccer demonstrations and clinics to young players in several countries. Pelé really enjoyed the experience and felt that he was providing a valuable contribution to the sport of soccer.

As Pelé's attitude improved in 1972, his goal total increased to fifty for the year. Toward the end of that season, Pelé signed a final two-year contract with Santos. He made it clear that he intended to end his playing career when the contract expired in 1974. Some members of the Brazilian media criticized Pelé, claiming that he wanted too much money and special treatment from the team. In response to this, Pelé decided to give his whole salary for the last year of his career with Santos to children's charities.

In 1973, Pelé continued trying to promote soccer around the world by giving a skills clinic in the United States. Pelé was very impressed by the number of eager young soccer fans who came to the clinic. The experience showed him that interest in soccer was growing among Americans. "To see many youngsters come to an outing like this is overwhelming," he said. "I just hope that I will get another chance to give them a clinic soon and I certainly hope I can do something to help that interest continue to grow."[42]

Pelé went on to lead Santos to the Brazilian professional league championship in 1973. He scored a remarkable fifty goals in his 17th professional soccer season. "Contemporary soccer superstars never reach even fifty goals a season," former U.S. Secretary of State Henry Kissinger declared. "For Pelé, who had thrice scored more than 100 goals a year, it signaled retirement."[43]

Noticing Problems with Brazilian Soccer

Pelé's role as a representative for soccer around the world gave him access to many other soccer organizations and leagues. This increased his awareness of various problems that affected soccer in Brazil. For example, the Brazilian professional leagues were made up of teams owned by wealthy and powerful football clubs. Under this system, individual players had very little control over their careers. They could be sold or traded to another club at a moment's notice, regardless of their level of experience or years of service. In addition, players who suffered career-ending injuries were often abandoned by their teams. The clubs did not provide insurance or make any type of payments to help players in this situation.

Throughout the early 1970s, Pelé worked with a group of soccer players to try to get basic labor protections for professional soccer players in Brazil. They tried to give veteran players more say in decisions about where and when they could be traded, for example, and they tried to arrange compensation for injured players. Some people criticized Pelé's attempts to secure better rights for soccer players in Brazil's professional leagues. Some questioned why he had waited until the end of his career to take a stand on the issue, while others claimed that his suggestions would cause financial harm to the football clubs.

As the issue of Pelé's relationship with Santos and his involvement in labor issues developed, it became clear that many fans still felt angry at Pelé for his refusal to play for Brazil in the 1974 World Cup tournament. He came under increasing pressure from fans, the media, and even the Brazilian government as the date of the tournament approached. The president of Brazil and a number

The Jules Rimet Cup was Brazil's to keep when the team won the third World Cup.

of high-ranking government officials even made a personal visit to Pelé's business offices to try to persuade him to change his mind and represent his country. When it became clear that Pelé planned to stick to his decision not to play, a group of bitter Brazilian fans fired gunshots through a window of his home. Pelé was outraged that anyone would endanger his family to express their feelings about his refusal to play in a soccer tournament. "I couldn't believe that people would be so upset, when I had only reaffirmed the decision I gave to them almost three years earlier,"[44] he stated.

Pelé went to the 1974 World Cup tournament, held in West Germany, but only as an interested observer. In recognition of his role in winning three world titles for Brazil, he was invited to take part in the opening ceremonies. Pelé accepted the Jules Rimet Trophy, which now belonged permanently to Brazil, from Uwe Seeler—a former captain of the West German team and the only player besides Pelé ever to score a goal in four different World Cup tournaments. In exchange, Pelé presented Seeler with the new trophy that would be awarded to future champions, the FIFA Cup.

Once the tournament got underway, Pelé watched from the stands as Brazil struggled to a fourth-place finish. In interviews afterward, Pelé said that he did not believe if he had played it would have changed the outcome for the national team. He noted that Brazil had lost a number of other key players from the 1970 championship squad to retirement or injury, including Tostão and Clodoaldo. He also felt that the Brazilian team had made a major error by using a defensive style of play that was not well suited to its strengths.

Saying Farewell to Santos

Following their country's disappointing performance in the 1974 World Cup, many Brazilian soccer fans turned their attention to Pelé's approaching retirement from Santos. Although many people tried to convince him to return for another year, Pelé insisted that the 1974 season would be the last of his playing career. "I am about to become Mr. Edson Arantes do Nascimento, an industrialist, an average father, and a husband," he declared. "This is my ambition, and nothing will change my mind right now."[45] Pelé claimed that he would limit his future involvement in soccer to teaching clinics for children, scouting young talent for Santos and the Brazilian National Team, and playing in an occasional charity benefit match.

Pelé appeared in forty-four games during his final season with Santos. He scored nineteen goals, including the 1,200th of his career. As the season entered its final weeks, Santos officials began promoting each match as Pelé's last with the team. While this made sure that Santos played all of its games in front of full crowds, it also created feelings of disappointment and disgust among many fans. After all, they paid a premium for tickets in the belief that they would see Pelé's farewell game, so they felt cheated when Pelé took the field again the following week.

Pelé's actual retirement from Santos took place on October 2, 1974. In his final match, Santos faced Ponte Preta at Maracaná Stadium. Pelé was surprised by the powerful emotions he felt during the game. After twenty minutes of play, he decided to do something memorable as a way of thanking the fans for their support. "I caught the ball in my hands—the ultimate in football movements to startle a crowd—and I could hear a sharp gasp of astonishment from the packed stadium. I ran with the ball to the center of the field, placed it on the center spot, and knelt, my knees on either side of the ball," he remembered. "The tears were running down my cheeks without control. The crowd realized what I was doing; they realized I was honoring them for the years they had honored me. They came to their feet with a roar."[46]

Pelé tried to run a ceremonial lap around the field, but he was overcome by emotion and had to run back to the locker room instead. Even after showering and getting dressed, he still felt unable to meet with reporters and give interviews. He ended up going home to be with his family. Although Pelé had not scored a goal in his final match, he had once again given all of himself to his many fans. People across Brazil felt sad to see his legendary career come to an end, but they reluctantly accepted his decision.

Choosing a New Path

In the months following his final game for Santos, Pelé mostly concentrated on his business interests, which now included clothing lines, sporting goods, coffee, and rubber products. But he also remained determined to find ways to promote soccer around the world, especially in countries where the sport had not yet achieved widespread popularity.

In Pelé's view, the United States was the greatest possible growth opportunity for soccer. Although the American people loved to watch and play sports, they did not pay much attention to soccer at that time. Soccer came far below the four major U.S. professional sports—baseball, football, basketball, and hockey—in terms of popularity and the number of young people taking part. A professional soccer league had been introduced in the United States in the early 1970s, but none of the teams managed to attract more than a few thousand people per game. Since the United States had never taken a team to the World Cup tournament, many Americans thought soccer was a foreign sport.

Pelé was sad about this situation. He wanted to make a difference by sharing the joy and excitement of his beloved game of soccer with the American people. In early 1975, Pelé began to seriously think about a plan that would help him achieve this goal. He started talks with the New York Cosmos, a team in the young North American Soccer League (NASL), about coming out of retirement and playing soccer in the United States.

Making a Tough Decision

Pelé had received an offer from the Cosmos several years earlier. Clive Toye, an English soccer writer who was coach and president of the New York team, had looked for Pelé after a Santos exhibition match in Jamaica. Toye had tried to persuade Pelé to play for the Cosmos, telling him that—as the biggest star in the sport—he could bring instant success to the team and the league. At the time, though, Pelé refused. He had received many offers over the years to play for some of the best teams in Europe, but he had turned them all down to remain in Brazil. When Toye first approached him, Pelé felt there was no reason for him to think about playing for a lesser team in the United States.

Over the next few years, however, Toye kept in touch with Pelé and became friends with many people close to him, including his brother Zoca and his former trainer Mazzei. Once Pelé retired from Santos, these trusted advisors encouraged him to think about resuming his playing career in the United States. If Pelé joined the Cosmos, they pointed out, he could achieve his dream of raising awareness of the sport of soccer among the American people. The New York team was also owned by Warner Communications, an important company in the American film, music, and publishing industries. They realized an association with Warner could be very good for Pelé in terms of business opportunities in entertainment and product endorsements. Finally, they pointed out that the NASL played a much shorter season than the Brazilian professional soccer leagues, which would allow Pelé to continue to focus on his business and family interests.

Growing Concerns

Despite all these factors favoring the Cosmos, Pelé still had a number of concerns about playing in the United States. For example, he worried that Brazilian soccer fans would react angrily to his decision to come out of retirement and continue his playing career outside of his home country. He thought many people would feel that he had betrayed their loyalty and trust. Pelé also worried that the Brazilian government—which had long ago called him a national treasure to prevent him from leaving the country—would not support his plan. Finally, Pelé worried about moving his wife and children to the United States. They would have to leave friends and family in Brazil and they would have to learn to speak a new language.

Fortunately for the Cosmos, Pelé's wife Rosemeri loved New York City and felt that it offered great educational opportunities for their children. Then U.S. Secretary of State Henry Kissinger—a huge soccer fan—also helped smooth over any hard feelings among leaders in the Brazilian government. Kissinger sent a letter to the president of Brazil expressing his view that allowing Pelé to play soccer in the United States "will substantially contribute to closer ties between Brazil and the U.S. in the field of sports."[47] Although Pelé knew that some Brazilian soccer fans would not like his decision to play elsewhere, he also realized that many others would appreciate his efforts to act as a representative for soccer and for Brazil.

Secretary of State Henry Kissinger was a great fan of soccer and Pelé.

Although Pelé's worries were resolved, and he still had a great desire to contribute to the development of soccer in the United States, the deciding factor turned out to be money. Once again, Pelé had neglected his business matters and had allowed serious problems to develop in one of the companies he owned. Although Pelé had enough money to pay off the company's debts, he knew that paying the debts out of his savings would be a major financial setback for his family.

The Cosmos offered him $7 million for three years—a higher salary than any contract Pelé had signed during his career with Santos—plus the money he earned in endorsements through Warner Communications. Pelé knew that signing this contract would enable him to pay off his debts comfortably. In addition, he felt that he could use the six-month NASL off-season to study the English language and American business management techniques.

In June 1975, after months of consideration, Pelé shocked many people around the world by announcing his decision to come out of retirement and play for the New York Cosmos. "Association football—soccer—is the most widely played game in the world—except in the United States," he explained. "It is my hope that I can help to make this game, which I love so much, as important a sport here as it is in the rest of the world."[48]

Joining the New York Cosmos

Pelé joined the Cosmos midway through the 1975 NASL season. Just as he and team organizers had hoped, Pelé's arrival in New York attracted a great deal of media attention. In fact, soccer became front-page news across America in the days leading up to his first game in a Cosmos uniform.

By the time Pelé took the field with his new team, the Cosmos had struggled to a 3–6 record. Pelé found that most of his teammates

Pelé joined the New York Cosmos in order to help the young sport of soccer in the United States.

did not have very much talent or experience. But he was eager to share both his skills and his enthusiasm, and his contributions helped the team post a 7–6 record over the remainder of the season. With Pelé appearing in the lineup, the Cosmos' average attendance was also boosted from 8,000 to 20,000 spectators per game. Pelé scored fifteen goals in twenty-three games during the 1975 season, which included a post-season exhibition tour of Europe and several nations in the Caribbean.

In 1976, the Cosmos hired a new coach who made several changes to the team's lineup and encouraged a defensive style of play. Pelé found these changes frustrating and felt that the coach did not make the best possible use of his skills. But the Cosmos' record improved to 16–8 for the year. The team qualified for the NASL playoffs but lost in the first round to the league-leading Tampa Bay Rowdies. Pelé contributed twenty-six goals that year.

As the 1977 season approached, the Cosmos added several high-profile international players to the team, including Franz Beckenbauer of West Germany, Giorgio Chinaglia of Italy, and Rildo of Brazil. Clive Toye argued that it was Pelé's decision to come to New York that helped the team to attract such talent. "Pelé had to be the first," he stated. "The other great players around the world [had] to say to themselves, 'If he trusts them, I have to trust them.'"[49]

A Change of Direction

During the first half of the 1977 season, all the new players on the Cosmos struggled to get along and play together as a team. As the season passed the halfway point, however, the team started coming together and began winning. "We've stopped playing as individuals," Chinaglia noted. "There has been a definite change of attitude on this club."[50] Several players mentioned Pelé's good example in explaining the team's newfound success. "The thing I admire most about Pelé is his sincerity, integrity, and dedication to the game," said Cosmos goalkeeper Shep Messing. "Never giving up, never coasting, trying harder than a rookie."[51]

The Cosmos advanced through the NASL playoffs to the league championship game, where they faced the Seattle Sounders. The match was played in front of 77,000 people—the largest crowd ever to watch soccer in North America—and televised across the United States and in a dozen other countries around the world. The two teams treated fans to an intense battle, which the Cosmos finally won by a score of 2–1. At the end of the game, Cosmos captain Werner Roth said, "Pelé is number one and now we are number one along with him. This team showed a lot of character."[52]

Saying One Last Goodbye

Pelé was thrilled to lead the Cosmos to the NASL championship. He felt that this achievement provided a perfect ending for his career. "I stop too high to give myself a chance to come down again," he explained. "You want to stop at the top. You go past, you are nothing but sad."[53]

The Cosmos honored Pelé's retirement from soccer by arranging a special exhibition match with Santos, his former team. The big event became one of the hottest tickets in sports, and the 75,000 available seats sold out six weeks in advance. The game took place on October 1, 1977, at the Meadowlands in New Jersey. In addition to a full crowd, it attracted 650 journalists from all over the

U.S. Experience Teaches Pelé the Secrets to Business Success

One of the reasons that Pelé agreed to play professional soccer in the United States was that he wanted to learn about American business management practices. By attending college courses and consulting with professionals in various industries, he came to understand some of the mistakes he had made in his early business career. "I was very sentimental; I did everything with my heart, and I lost a lot of money," he acknowledged. "The Americans taught me that you can't let your emotions get in the way. You can't make a decision with your heart. You can't do business to help someone. You can't do business with members of your family…. Business is business. You have to be tough."

Pelé, "On a New Kick," *Time*, October 8, 2001.

On October 1, 1977, Pelé played his last match in an exhibition match between the Cosmos and Santos.

world. It was broadcast live on television throughout the United States and in thirty-eight other countries.

Before the match started, Pelé stepped onto the field and made a speech encouraging people to support one of his favorite causes: children's welfare. "I want to take this opportunity to ask you to pay attention to the young of the world, the children," he told the crowd. "We need them too much…. Love is more important that what we can take in life."[54] Then Pelé led the packed stadium in a thunderous chant of "Love! Love! Love!"

Once the match got underway, Pelé scored a goal for New York in the first half. At halftime, he presented his Cosmos jersey to his father, Dondinho, in a special ceremony. Then Pelé put on a Santos jersey and played the second half with his former team. The fans who watched this historic match really did witness Pelé's final game. Unlike his earlier decisions to retire, he never reconsidered this one. Although Pelé was often spotted at Cosmos games over the next few years, he always watched the action from the sidelines or the stands. But of course, the end of Pelé's playing career did not mark the end of his contributions to the sport of soccer.

Introducing Soccer to America

By the time Pelé played his last game, it was already clear that he had achieved his goal of increasing awareness of soccer and its popularity in the United States. The number of players registered with the U.S. Soccer Association increased from 100,000 to 400,000 during his time with the Cosmos. This rapid rise made soccer the fastest-growing team sport in the United States in the late 1970s. "I didn't expect this so quickly," Pelé acknowledged. "I thought it would take a few more years. But everybody wants to come now. The kids bring soccer here. The kids know it is a great game."[55]

Film Describes Pelé's Impact on Soccer in the United States

In 2006, a documentary film was released that covers the remarkable final chapter of Pelé's soccer career. *Once in a Lifetime: The Extraordinary Story of the New York Cosmos* describes the 1977 season, when Pelé led the Cosmos to the North American Soccer League championship. It also describes the many ways in which Pelé's decision to cap off his career in New York generated excitement about soccer throughout the United States. For example, attending Cosmos games became a favorite activity for lots of celebrities and politicians during the summer of 1977. Participation in American youth soccer leagues also increased dramatically around this time. In a review for *Interview* magazine, Brendan Lemon called the film—which was directed by Paul Crowder and narrated by Matt Dillon—"an entertaining look at a barely remembered chapter in sports history."

Brendan Lemon, "Review: *Once in a Lifetime*," *Interview*, July 2006, p. 38.

Pelé has made soccer important here [in the United States]. Babe Ruth did that for baseball, Jack Dempsey for boxing, Bobby Jones for golf. And now, half a century later, Pelé has done it for soccer.

Dave Anderson, "Pelé's Legacy: The Game and the Man," *New York Times*, August 28, 1977, p. 166.

Most importantly, Pelé helped change the attitudes of many Americans about soccer. "It's in the infant stage of a boom that may leave it unmatched among team sports in this country," declared a writer for the *New York Times*. "It is no longer an 'immigrant' sport but suddenly something as American as, say, baseball."[56]

Pelé felt very proud of his success in promoting soccer in America. "I believe that the beautiful game of soccer has arrived in the United States,"[57] he declared.

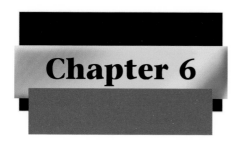

Global Ambassador for the "Beautiful Game"

Pelé ended his twenty-year professional soccer career on a triumphant note in 1977. He led the New York Cosmos to the North American Soccer League championship. And he also raised the level of interest and the number of people taking part in soccer throughout the United States. This experience encouraged Pelé to continue working to promote the "beautiful game" around the world following his retirement. Pelé remained a very visible and vocal representative for his beloved sport for the next three decades.

Using Soccer to Unite People

By the time Pelé retired from the Cosmos, he was one of the most famous and respected athletes in the world. Pelé's fame and popularity created a number of opportunities for him to become involved in the field of entertainment. In 1977 he published an autobiography, *My Life and the Beautiful Game*. He also appeared

Pelé wrote his autobiography, My Life and the Beautiful Game, *and appeared in the film version of his life story,* Pelé.

in the film version of his life story, called *Pelé*, and wrote all the music for the film's soundtrack. Pelé also starred alongside Michael Caine and Sylvester Stallone in the 1981 film *Victory*, which follows a multinational group of soccer players who try to escape from a prison camp during World War II.

Pelé's book and movie deals, together with his ongoing business interests and endorsement contracts, enabled him to earn millions of dollars each year. Nevertheless, he remained the same simple, humble man who enjoyed sharing his genuine love for soccer with his many fans. "Fame and money haven't changed Pelé," declared a writer for the *New York Times*.

> He has a warm and pleasant smile and is generous with his most valuable possession, himself. He will sign autographs until his arm tires, pose ungrudgingly for pictures, and talk as if the interviewer was doing him a favor.[58]

Pelé realized that his worldwide fame came with important responsibilities. He knew that he served as a role model for many young fans, and he was determined to represent the positive values of hard work, fair play, and the pure joy of competition. "Every kid in the world who plays football wants to be Pelé—which means I have the responsibility of showing them how to be a footballer but also how to be a man,"[59] he acknowledged.

Above all, Pelé hoped to use his popularity to bring people together and make the world a better place. "It seems that God brought me to earth with a mission to unite people—never to separate them,"[60] he stated. "I would like to be remembered as a person who showed the world that the simplicity of a man is still the most important quality. Through simplicity and sincerity, you can pull all humankind together."[61]

Pelé used the sport of soccer to try to bring people together. "Because of its universal appeal, I believe soccer can unite all the peoples of the world. Its theme is so vast it can fill the world with understanding, peace, and love," he explained. "All these years in

Pelé starred with Michael Caine (shown here with director John Huston) and Sylvester Stallone in the film Victory.

Pelé Appears in *Victory*

After his soccer career ended, Pelé took advantage of his worldwide popularity to become an actor. His best-known film appearance came in the 1981 movie *Victory*, which was directed by John Huston and also starred Michael Caine and Sylvester Stallone.

This action-adventure movie centers around a diverse group of Allied soldiers who are being held in a prisoner-of-war camp in Nazi Germany during World War II. When a German officer invites the soldiers to form a soccer team and play an exhibition match against the German national team in Paris, they must decide whether to play the match or use it as an opportunity to escape.

Pelé played the role of Luis Fernandez, a South American soccer star who joins the Allied team. In a review of *Victory* for the *New York Times*, Vincent Canby noted that in the exciting final match, Pelé "supplies the film with a couple of tantalizing glimpses of the talent that made him the legend he is."

Directed by John Huston, Victory *starred Pelé, Michael Caine, and Sylvester Stallone.*

Victory remains popular among soccer fans. In fact, according to the footymania.com Web site, the movie won the title of Best Football Film of All Time in a 2004 poll of European soccer fans.

Vincent Canby, "Caine and Stallone in Huston's *Victory*," *New York Times*, July 31, 1981; "Footymania Football Movies: *Victory*," available online at http://www.footymania.com/movies.phtml.

soccer, I have come to realize that through soccer we can all be brothers. Soccer's appeal and magnitude is such that it ignores race, religion, and politics. Soccer has one real goal and that is to create friendship."[62] To achieve his goal, Pelé traveled all over the world promoting soccer through public appearances, clinics, and demonstrations.

Bringing the World Cup to America

Pelé's attempts to develop soccer around the world brought him many fans and admirers. In 1978, he earned the International Peace Award for his efforts to improve relations between people in different countries. Unfortunately for Pelé, though, the constant travel had a negative impact on his personal life. He and his wife Rosemeri separated in 1978 after twelve years of marriage, and they were divorced in 1982.

Pelé suffered another disappointment in 1985, when his former team, the New York Cosmos, was forced to shut down. After winning a second NASL title in 1978, the Cosmos had started to go downhill. Fans stopped going to games, and the team had to deal with financial hardships. Pelé blamed the problems, which affected the entire league, on owners' attempts to expand too rapidly. "Soccer became too big too fast," he noted. "[The NASL] had eighteen teams in 1977, and it was very balanced. Then they opened it up to twenty-four teams the next year, and it was not balanced anymore."[63]

Although professional soccer did not last long in the United States without Pelé, his influence was still felt in other areas during the 1980s and 1990s. The number of children taking part in soccer continued to increase in communities across the country, and more American colleges and universities offered varsity soccer programs. In addition, many Americans started paying greater attention to international soccer events, such as the Olympic Games and the World Cup tournament.

When the NASL went out of business, Pelé became the most important spokesman for the movement to bring the World Cup soccer tournament to the United States. Pelé had a number of reasons to support the U.S. bid to host the premier event in international soccer. First, he believed that holding World Cup games in the United States would continue to increase Americans' interest and participation in soccer. Second, he felt that the United States was in a stronger economic position to host the tournament than most other countries.

In 1988, Pelé argued that the United States should be selected to host the 1994 tournament instead of the other finalists, Morocco and Brazil. His support for the U.S. bid upset many Brazilians, who

The 1994 World Cup

In 1994, the World Cup was held in the United States for the first time, in part because of Pelé's promotional efforts.

Thanks in part to Pelé's promotional efforts, the World Cup soccer tournament was held in the United States for the first time in 1994. It turned out to be one of the most successful tournaments in history. In a country not known for its interest in soccer, average attendance for the fifty-two matches was 69,000, which set a new World Cup record.

The final match between Brazil and Italy was watched on television by an estimated 1.2 billion fans around the world, including 10 million in the United States. The popularity of the first U.S. World Cup led to the creation of a new American professional soccer league, Major League Soccer (MLS), which made its debut in 1996 with ten teams.

felt that he was being disloyal to his home country. Pelé claimed that Brazil faced too many economic problems to finance the World Cup. "A country where millions of people are starving and which has the Third World's largest foreign debt cannot consider the sponsorship of a World Cup with government money,"[64] he stated.

Thanks in part to Pelé's support, FIFA officials did select the United States to host the 1994 World Cup. And most Brazilian fans happily forgot about the issue when Brazil went on to win the tournament.

Fighting the System in Brazil

Around the time that the United States hosted its first World Cup, Pelé remarried. He and his second wife, the Brazilian journalist Assiria Seixas Lemos, eventually had two children together.

In 1995, the president of Brazil invited Pelé to serve in the government as minister of sports. Pelé welcomed this opportunity to tackle what he thought were serious problems in Brazil's system of professional soccer. Pelé had long believed that the professional football clubs held too much power over the lives of players. He knew that professional soccer raised billions of dollars in revenue each year in Brazil. But most of this money went straight into the pockets of wealthy club owners, and only a small percentage went to the men who actually played the sport.

As Brazil's sports minister, Pelé took a number of steps to change the professional football leagues and make changes that benefit the players. For example, he suggested a law—which became known as the Pelé Law—to eliminate bribery and corruption among football club owners by introducing inspections of a team's financial records.

Although Pelé's efforts as sports minister brought him a lot of support from soccer fans and the Brazilian media, they also earned him some powerful enemies. When the wealthy team owners and officials found their interests were threatened, they responded by refusing to do business with Pelé's sporting goods and sports marketing companies. Pelé's businesses suffered as a result.

Both during and after his service as Brazil's minister of sports, Pelé also tried to tackle what he thought were major problems in international soccer. For example, he encouraged FIFA to change some rules that would increase scoring in matches. Pelé realized that the average number of goals scored per World Cup match went down with every tournament, and that many matches ended in scoreless ties and had to be decided through penalty-kick shootouts.

In speeches and interviews throughout the 1990s, Pelé argued that rule changes were needed to encourage teams to move away from rough, defensive play toward more creative, offensive play. "Defense no longer merely has the upper hand, it has a stranglehold on the game," he argued. "It is goals that have made soccer the world's most popular game, not scoreless ties that are decided by penalty kicks.... What has been lost in the process is the very heart and soul of the game—creativity."[65] Although Pelé's efforts were not always popular, he felt a great responsibility to defend the standard of soccer in Brazil and internationally.

International Awards

Pelé received many honors and awards in recognition of his tireless work on behalf of the world's children and his contributions to the sport of soccer. In 1995, for example, the United Nations Educational, Scientific, and Cultural Organization (UNESCO) named him a Goodwill Ambassador. Two years later, the Queen of England made him an honorary Knight of the British Empire.

Good Will

Pelé has done more good will than all the ambassadors of the world put together.

J. B. Pinheiro, Brazil's Ambassador to the United States, quoted in Alex Yannis, "Pelé's Legacy to His Fans: Nobody Did It Better," *New York Times*, October 2, 1977, p. S3.

The turn of the twenty-first century brought Pelé a great deal of recognition as one of the top athletes of the past hundred years. The International Olympic Committee named him Athlete of the Century, for example. And he was named Footballer of the Century by FIFA. One of Pelé's biggest honors came in 2000, when he received the prestigious Laureus World Sports Award for Lifetime Achievement from one of his heroes, former South African President Nelson Mandela.

By the 2000s, Pelé earned an estimated $30 million a year from his businesses and endorsement contracts. He appeared in advertisements for such international companies as MasterCard,

Many awards were given to Pelé in recognition of his contributions to the sport of soccer, including Athlete of the Century.

Pepsi, Procter and Gamble, and Pfizer. He also continued to perform public service work for UNICEF and other children's organizations.

In 2003, the Brazilian state of São Paulo opened a museum honoring Pelé in Santos. The items on display at the facility included a radio set belonging to Pelé's father, various trophies and game balls, telegrams of congratulations from world leaders, and personal photographs. In 2006, Pelé published an updated autobiography entitled *Pelé: The Autobiography*. He also served as the subject of a 720-page book called *Pelé: Edson Arantes do Nascimento*. This work contains 1,700 pictures documenting his career, articles by numerous sportswriters, and interviews with many of his friends, family members, and former teammates.

Instant Recognition

Pelé's name still sparks instant recognition from even the youngest fans, and mention of it to anyone above the age of thirty is greeted with a misty-eyed respect afforded only to a very select band of modern sporting heroes.

"Pelé Still in Global Demand," available online at http://www.sportsillustrated.cnn.com/soccer/world/2002/world_cup/news/2002/05/29/pele_icon/.

Even though 2007 marked the thirtieth anniversary of the end of Pelé's legendary playing career, he continued to attract interest and appreciation among soccer fans around the world. Pelé continued to serve as a global representative for soccer, the "beautiful game" that became his lifelong passion. "There is nothing like soccer," he declared. "Full stadium, thousands of banners. The ball shining white, ahead. A sure kick. Goal. That to me is everything an athlete can ever want."[66]

Notes

Introduction: The King of Soccer
1. "Soccer's Superlative: Edson Arantes do Nascimento," *New York Times,* June 4, 1975, p. 30.
2. "Pelé," *The International Football Hall of Fame,* 2000. Available online at http://www.ihof.com/hof/pele.asp.
3. Alex Bellos, *Futebol: Soccer, the Brazilian Way.* New York and London: Bloomsbury, 2002, p. 115.
4. Quoted in E. M. Swift, "A Dream Come True." *Sports Illustrated,* June 20, 1994, p. 86.

Chapter 1: Talent Overcomes Obstacles
5. Quoted in Alex Yannis, "Pelé to Play Soccer Here for $7 Million," *New York Times,* June 4, 1975, p. 1.
6. Pelé, with Robert L. Fish, *My Life and the Beautiful Game: The Autobiography of Pelé.* Garden City, New York: Doubleday, 1977, p. 16.
7. Pelé, *My Life and the Beautiful Game,* p. 14.
8. Quoted in Joe Marcus, *The World of Pelé.* New York: Mason/Charter, 1976, p. 9.
9. Quoted in Marcus, *The World of Pelé,* p. 11.
10. Pelé, *My Life and the Beautiful Game,* p. 25.
11. Pelé, *My Life and the Beautiful Game,* p. 84.
12. Pelé, *My Life and the Beautiful Game,* p. 91.
13. Quoted in James Hahn and Lynn Hahn, *Pelé! The Sports Career of Edson do Nascimento.* New York: Crestwood House, 1981.

Chapter 2: Teenage Sensation Wins First World Cup
14. Pelé, *My Life and the Beautiful Game,* p. 120.
15. Quoted in Marcus, *The World of Pelé,* p. 27.
16. Pelé, *My Life and the Beautiful Game,* p. 41.
17. Ian Thomsen, "A Great Revelation Was Afoot," *Sports Illustrated,* November 29, 1999, p. 36.

18. Quoted in Marcus, *The World of Pelé*, p. 30.
19. Pelé, *My Life and the Beautiful Game,* p. 49.
20. "Pelé: Brazil's Beautiful Star above All Others." *Classic Moments from FIFA World Cup History.* Available online at http://fifaworldcup.yahoo.com/06/en/p/cp/bra/pele.html.
21. Quoted in Marcus, *The World of Pelé*, p. 32.
22. "Brazil Gains World's Cup." *New York Times*, June 30, 1958, p. 28.
23. Quoted in Marcus, *The World of Pelé,* p. 37.

Chapter 3: Sidelined by Rough Play
24. Pelé, *My Life and the Beautiful Game,* p. 170.
25. Quoted in Marcus, *The World of Pelé*, p. 42.
26. Quoted in Marcus, *The World of Pelé*, p. 50.
27. Pelé, *My Life and the Beautiful Game,* p. 189.
28. "Rough Tactics in Cup Tourney Put World Soccer on Defensive," *New York Times*, July 25, 1966, p. 31.
29. Quoted in Marcus, *The World of Pelé*, p. 61.
30. Pelé, *My Life and the Beautiful Game,* p. 196.

Chapter 4: Coming Back for Another World Cup Triumph
31. "Pelé Becomes First Modern Player to Reach 1,000 Goals," *New York Times*, November 20, 1969, p. 65.
32. Quoted in "Pelé," *The International Football Hall of Fame.*
33. Quoted in Marcus, *The World of Pelé*, p. 100.
34. Bellos, *Futebol: Soccer, the Brazilian Way*, p. 44.
35. Pelé, *My Life and the Beautiful Game,* p. 245.
36. Bellos, *Futebol: Soccer, the Brazilian Way*, p. 44.
37. Quoted in Marcus, *The World of Pelé*, p. 105.
38. Quoted in "Pelé: Brazil's Beautiful Star above All Others," *Classic Moments from FIFA World Cup History.*
39. Quoted in "Pelé: Brazil's Beautiful Star above All Others," *Classic Moments from FIFA World Cup History.*
40. Quoted in Marcus, *The World of Pelé,* p. 108.
41. Quoted in "…And Pele Departs the World Stage," *New York Times*, July 19, 1971, p. 19.

Chapter 5: Bringing Soccer to America

42. Quoted in Marcus, *The World of Pelé,* p. 132.
43. Quoted in Henry A. Kissinger, "The Phenomenon: Pelé," *Time,* June 14, 1999, p. 110.
44. Quoted in Marcus, *The World of Pelé,* p. 136.
45. Quoted in Marcus, *The World of Pelé,* p. 138.
46. Pelé, *My Life and the Beautiful Game,* p. 281.
47. Quoted in Yannis, "Pelé to Play Soccer Here for $7 Million."
48. Pelé, *My Life and the Beautiful Game,* p. 292.
49. Quoted in Alex Yannis, "Jealousy Gives Way to Joy among the Surging Cosmos," *New York Times,* June 12, 1977, p. 177.
50. Quoted in Alex Yannis, "Pelé's Legacy to His Fans: Nobody Did It Better," *New York Times,* October 2, 1977, p. S3.
51. Quoted in Alex Yannis, "Cosmos Win Soccer Title," *New York Times,* August 29, 1977, p. 1.
52. Quoted in Tony Kornheiser, "A New and Different Life for Pelé," *New York Times,* May 21, 1978, p. S1.
53. Quoted in *New York Times,* October 2, 1977.
54. Quoted in Anderson, "Pelé's Legacy."
55. Dave Anderson, "Pelé's Legacy: The Game and the Man," *New York Times,* August 28, 1977, p. 166.
56. Tony Kornheiser, "Americans Have Adopted Soccer, No Longer an 'Immigrant' Sport," *New York Times,* July 5, 1977, p. 61.
57. Pelé, "Pelé's Farewell: What Soccer Has Meant," *New York Times,* September 25, 1977, p. 176.

Chapter 6: Global Ambassador for the "Beautiful Game"

58. "Soccer's Superlative: Edson Arantes do Nascimento," *New York Times.*
59. Quoted in "Pelé: Brazil's Beautiful Star above All Others," *Classic Moments from FIFA World Cup History.*
60. Pelé. "Pelé's Farewell: What Soccer Has Meant."
61. Quoted in Yannis, "Pelé's Legacy to His Fans: Nobody Did It Better."

62. Pelé, "Pelé's Farewell: What Soccer Has Meant."
63. Quoted in E. M. Swift, "A Dream Come True."
64. Quoted in E. M. Swift, "A Dream Come True."
65. Pelé, "Let's Put the Sock Back into Soccer." *Sports Illustrated,* March 25, 1991, p. 82.
66. Quoted in Marcus, *The World of Pelé,* p. 121.

Important Dates

1940
Pelé is born as Edson Arantes do Nascimento on October 23 in Tres Coracoes, Brazil.

1954
Former Brazilian soccer star Waldemar de Brito recognizes Pelé's talent and recruits him to play in a youth league.

1956
Pelé joins the Santos professional soccer team in Brazil.

1958
Pelé leads Brazil's national soccer team to its first FIFA World Cup championship.

1961
The president of Brazil officially declares Pelé a national treasure in order to prevent him from playing soccer in another country.

1962
Brazil wins a second World Cup title without the help of Pelé, who is sidelined by injury in the first match of the tournament.

1966
Brazil is knocked out of the World Cup tournament after Pelé suffers a leg injury.

1969
Pelé reaches an important milestone by scoring the 1,000th goal of his legendary career.

1970
Pelé helps Brazil become the first nation ever to claim three World Cup titles.

1971

Pelé retires from the Brazilian national soccer team.

1974

Pelé retires from Santos, his longtime Brazilian professional team.

1975

Pelé agrees to play for the New York Cosmos in the young North American Soccer League.

1977

Pelé retires from soccer following an exhibition match attended by 76,000 fans. He publishes an autobiography, *My Life and the Beautiful Game,* and composes the soundtrack for a film about his career, called *Pelé.*

1995

Pelé is named Brazil's minister of sports.

2000

Pelé receives the prestigious Laureus Sports Award for Lifetime Achievement. He is also named FIFA Footballer of the Century.

For More Information

Books

Joe Marcus, *The World of Pelé*. New York: Mason/Charter, 1976. Based on public sources as well as interviews with some of Pelé's friends and teammates, this readable biography is an account of Pelé's early life and career up to his 1975 decision to join the New York Cosmos.

Pelé, with Robert L. Fish, *My Life and the Beautiful Game: The Autobiography of Pelé*. Garden City, New York: Doubleday, 1977. Pelé offers an honest and in-depth account of his youth and development as a soccer player, as well as his World Cup triumphs and disappointments.

Pelé, with Orlando Duarte and Alex Bellos, *Pelé: The Autobiography*. London: Simon and Schuster, 2006. This updated autobiography recounts the highlights of Pelé's soccer career and also provides an entertaining, and often opinionated, look at his life since retirement.

Periodicals

Henry A. Kissinger, "The Phenomenon: Pelé," *Time*, June 14, 1999, p. 110. As part of the Time 100 series about the most influential people of the twentieth century, the former U.S. Secretary of State describes Pelé's impact as a soccer player and as a goodwill ambassador.

Pelé, "Pelé's Farewell: What Soccer Has Meant," *New York Times*, September 25, 1977, p. 176. Writing at the conclusion of his playing career, Pelé shares memories, thanks fans, and expresses his desire to promote the game of soccer.

"Soccer's Superlative: Edson Arantes do Nascimento," *New York Times*, June 4, 1975, p. 30. Published when Pelé agreed to play for the New York Cosmos, this article provides a glowing account of his early life and career.

E. M. Swift, "A Dream Come True," *Sports Illustrated,* June 20, 1994, p. 86. This article describes Pelé's many contributions to soccer, especially his successful effort to bring the World Cup tournament to the United States.

Internet Sources

FIFA World Cup (fifaworldcup.yahoo.com). This site provides detailed descriptions of Pelé's legendary World Cup performances in its Classic Moments from FIFA World Cup History section.

International Football Hall of Fame (www.ihof.com). This site includes a biographical profile of Pelé and statistical highlights of his career.

Index

Picture Credits

About the Author

Laurie Collier Hillstrom is a partner in Northern Lights Writers Group, a writing and editorial services firm based in Brighton, Michigan. She has written and edited award-winning reference works on a wide range of subjects, including American history, biography, popular culture, and international environmental issues.